At the Foot of the Cross

How to pray for healing and wholeness

For individuals, groups and churches

Dr Caris Grimes

malcolm down
PUBLISHING

Copyright © Dr Caris Grimes 2025

First published 2025 by Malcolm Down Publishing Ltd
www.malcolmdown.co.uk

28 27 26 25   7 6 5 4 3 2 1

The right of Dr Caris Grimes to be identified as the author of this work has been asserted by her in accordance with the Copyright, Designs and Patents Act 1988.

All rights reserved. No part of this publication may be reproduced, stored in a retrieval system, or transmitted in any other form or by any means, electronic, mechanical, photocopying, recording or otherwise, without the prior permission of the publisher.

British Library Cataloguing in Publication Data
A catalogue record for this book is available from the British Library.

ISBN 978-1-917455-15-2

Unless otherwise indicated, Scripture quotations are taken from the Holy Bible, New International Version (Anglicised edition).
Copyright ©1979, 1984, 2011 by Biblica.
Used by permission of Hodder & Stoughton Publishers, an Hachette UK company.
All rights reserved.
"NIV" is a registered trademark of Biblica.
UK trademark number 1448790.

Cover design by Esther Kotecha
Art direction by Sarah Grace

Printed in the UK

"The healing work of the Church is the process of being made whole *by* Christ, *for* Christ, *into* Christ"

Edgar Bell (1953)

What Others Are Saying About *At the Foot of the Cross*:

"There is a rising sense of expectation among those with their spiritual antenna up that God is re-gifting his people, particularly in the realm of healing in the name of Jesus. Caris Grimes' book is further evidence that although the healing ministry can get locked up by policies, protocols and performance, it is to ordinary believers that gifts of healing are given and, in my experience, in whose hands it is the most effective. The fact that Caris writes with a doctor's understanding as well as that of a 'prayer minister' is all the more compelling. This is a book that will challenge you but not frighten you. It will encourage you but not leave you complacent, but, above all, it will lead you into new adventures of faith."

Revd Wes Sutton
Director, Acorn Christian Healing Foundation

"Healing and wholeness should be at the heart of our everyday Christian experience. In a world with so much brokenness and so many seeking healing in body, mind and spirit this is a timely book. Caris' book is a vital companion not only on the journey to healing and wholeness but a closer walk with Jesus."

Bishop Mike Royal
General Secretary, Churches Together in England

I surely commend this really helpful book written by Caris Grimes who has real insight into the healing ministry. Who, as a surgeon, highlights that the Lord uses medics to bring healing but then acknowledges that the Lord Jesus also brings supernatural healing. The book is very well balanced, is biblically based and is an excellent introduction to healing and wholeness, constantly taking us back to scripture. This is a brilliant introduction to the healing ministry, and I would strongly recommend it to ministers and vicars to use in their churches to help congregations gain understanding of the healing ministry. It would be ideal for small group meetings to help understanding of Jesus' priority for healing and his care and compassion for the broken-hearted. I want to also commend all to read the quotes by Edgar Bell, the author's great-grandfather, who brings profound insight into the book.

Lieutenant Colonel Jan Ransom MBE
Founder and Director, Flame International

Foreword

Caris tenderly invites us to the foot of the cross – over six weeks of thoughtful and incisive studies, which draw holistically on her deep Christian faith and profession as a surgeon.

It is easy for the healing ministry of the people of God to be dried up to a tiny trickle, dammed in by questions of "Does God care?" in the face of unanswered prayer or "Is supernatural healing possible?" in a world of scientific advances. Caris carefully unblocks these dams and invites us to experience the depth and breadth of God's river of healing. For us. Today.

As I read this book, the image that came to mind is best summed up in the "Love Song of the Welsh Revival" hymn written by William Rees in the 19th century.

On the mount of crucifixion
Fountains opened deep and wide
Through the floodgates of God's mercy
Flowed a vast and gracious tide
Grace and love, like mighty rivers
Poured incessant from above
And heaven's peace and perfect justice
Kissed a guilty world in love

Caris gently keeps bringing us back to the foot of the cross. It is at the cross that Jesus' sacrificial death made healing and wholeness possible for the whole of creation. Not neat and tidy canals, but torrential rivers in flood, bursting their banks to drench the very fabric of society. Healing and deliverance, reconciliation and restoration in whole communities and spheres of influence.

Here's my unashamed agenda in agreeing with joy to write this foreword: I long for healing ministry to become normalised in Christian culture in the West in the 21st century.

A very formative influence on my Christian faith in early adulthood was a visit to India and then Kenya with my church in Cambridge who had developed friendly links with colleges that trained pastors in Hyderabad and Nakuru. One might have presumed that a bunch of us Cambridge graduates were helping out our brothers and sisters in the two-thirds world, who hadn't had the same privileged education as us. But the privilege was all theirs. I had never seen, never mind experienced for myself, someone healed in front of my eyes. Simply because I had prayed for them in the name of Jesus. This was everyday church life. In Nakuru, a blind woman received her sight. I remember arriving back at Gatwick airport, with such a disjunct in my faith. It seemed like Britain was covered in a "blanket of unbelief", as Leslie Newbiggin put it on his return from India. Seven years later, training to be a vicar in Oxford, I remember one tutorial on the gospels that ran on for twice its allocated time, when the lovely gentle academic suddenly swore at me in a response to something I'd casually said. "***t! – you believe in miracles – you're a scientist!" "Yes, of course I do – I've seen them." So much scholarship over the last two hundred years has air-brushed the possibility of miracles from our colour palette of possibilities. It's not black and white. There's plenty of grey areas where simple faith-filled prayers seem to go unanswered; but there's certainly more colourful answers than we imagine.

When my dad was given six weeks to live after his treatment for leukaemia failed, he and my mum happened to be passing a gazebo on the streets in Bolton advertising prayer for healing by local churches. In desperation, they called in. Something significant happened. He wasn't miraculously cured, but there was a notable measure of healing – he lived another 18 months. My mum said, "Why don't you advertise this more? Why don't you tell people that Jesus can heal today? Your churches would be full!"

As a bishop, I have lots of opportunities to pray for healing. I always ask Jesus. And I always ask big. My sense is God's answer never falls short of our asking, even if there isn't a cure this side of heaven. But if I were to recount the miraculous answers, this foreword would become very long indeed.

So dip your toes in this life-giving stream. Savour Caris' daily studies. Invite some friends to join in the group work. Take her sabbatical days to ponder and reflect. Reach for her practical advice to those working in healing professions.

Underpinning much of her writing, Caris draws on the deep wells of faith of her great-grandfather, Edgar Bell, who had an astonishing healing ministry as an Anglican priest in Liverpool. "So, then, we are both brought within the scope of the great Redemptive act, and since there is no more that I can do, I leave my patient there, at the foot of the Cross, asking nothing, but just placing him at God's disposal, who alone knows his need and who alone can adequately meet it" (Edgar Bell, *Redemptive Healing*).

So I hope you enjoy this book as much as I did. May it lead you to find healing at the foot of the cross in ways you couldn't possibly imagine. And there may you find a deep river "deep enough to swim in – a river that no one could cross" (Ezekiel 47:5).

Jill Duff
Anglican Bishop of Lancaster

Introduction

Why this book?

This book is written to encourage you to pray for the healing and wholeness of others. Many of us would like to have the courage to pray for others for healing and wholeness but we face obstacles and hurdles, fears and concerns that stop us doing so.

Firstly, there are things we don't understand. We hear of someone being miraculously cured of cancer but then when we pray for a friend in a similar position, nothing seems to happen. We struggle with the issues as to whether God really cares and, if he does, why he appears to stay silent in the face of suffering and illness. We may doubt whether he really exists and whether he really can and does still heal. We may have been left angry and frustrated with God for something that has happened in the past, for example a loved one who died too soon and despite so much prayer.

Secondly, we wonder whether we are really called to pray for others. If we have the courage to pray for others, we may lack the courage to pray with others, to place our hands on them and pray for their healing. We may fear the outcome or, rather, we fear the lack of outcome. We pray *for* others rather than *with* others, because then, if nothing appears to happen, it feels easier to bear. Maybe we wonder whether prayer for healing would be better left for those with a clear spiritual gift for it.

Thirdly, we wonder how to pray for others. We wonder where and when we should do it, whether we should put a hand on their shoulder, what words we should use. We wonder what may happen and then doubt that we have the skills to manage any of the possible consequences. We may have never prayed for someone like this and, simply, we aren't sure we have the courage to try alone.

This book is for you. It is also for your small group, your Christian book club and your church/organisation.

This book is written because we are all commissioned to pray for healing for others regardless of our spiritual gifting. This book is to give you the knowledge and skills you need to pray effectively and to encourage you to start trying no matter how inadequate you feel for the task.

For six days of each week we will explore a different topic and then do a prayer exercise. On the seventh day we will take a break and relax, refresh and rest with a psalm and, if you can manage it, some time in God's creation.

Learning to pray for others is sometimes better done within a group or as part of a wider organisation. Therefore, there are also group discussion questions at the end of each week.

Introduction

How the book works
The book is divided into three parts:

Part 1: Learning and praying. You can do this part as an individual, as part of a group or as a church. The first two weeks look at the theology of healing and suffering and help us to think about whether we have a God who cares and, if we do, why we don't always see physical healing when we pray. Weeks 3 and 4 look at how to pray with others.

Part 2: Organisational context. This part covers the role of the sacraments and services for healing. However, it also looks at critical issues of safety and risk, including consent, confidentiality, safeguarding, training and governance.

Part 3: Appendices. These include my own thoughts for those who work within the healing professions (I'm a consultant surgeon), along with suggested sermon outlines for church leaders, a list of the types of healing and a glossary of spiritual gifts.

Book quirks
Firstly, in this book I refer to suffering as it relates to sickness (physical, spiritual, mental and emotional) and personal brokenness. However, it is worth noting that when the Bible talks about suffering, it often refers to more than this. For example, when Paul boasts of his suffering in 2 Corinthians 11:16-33, he is referring to flogging and beatings, shipwrecks, hunger, thirst, being

cold and naked and daily pressure of concern for the churches.

Secondly, this topic crosses the entire breadth of church traditions and denominations. It is worth noting that historically, two of the main authors on the subject came from completely different church backgrounds. Francis MacNutt was a Roman Catholic priest, whereas John Wimber was a founding leader of the Vineyard movement. I have endeavoured to make this book ecumenical but inevitably my writing reflects my own assumptions and traditions, which I hope you will be patient with when they are not consistent with your own.

Thirdly, please note that unless otherwise stated, the quotes used are from the New International Version of the Bible. This is simply because it's a version that I personally am most familiar with. Please do look up alternative versions of the verses if it is helpful.

Finally, I will be using quotes from Edgar Bell's book *Redemptive Healing*. Edgar was my great-grandfather. He was an Anglican parish priest with a miraculous and powerful gift for healing. He also taught on the subject. I have taken the quotes from an original manuscript from talks he gave on healing in Liverpool in 1953, although a slightly different and more modernised version has been published and is in the "Further reading" section.

Contents

Part 1: Learning and Praying — 19

Week 1: Does God care? — 21
- Day 1: The foot of the cross — 23
- Day 2: The God who forgives — 27
- Day 3: The God who gives — 31
- Day 4: Suffering — 35
- Day 5: Why pray for the sick? — 39
- Day 6: The power of the resurrection — 43
- Day 7: Reflection — 47
- Week 1: Group discussion questions — 49

Week 2: Why don't we always see physical healing? — 51
- Day 1: God's priorities — 53
- Day 2: God's kingdom — 57
- Day 3: God's methods — 61
- Day 4: God's claim — 65
- Day 5: God's enemies — 69
- Day 6: God's perspective — 73
- Day 7: Reflection — 77
- Week 2: Group discussion questions — 79

Week 3: How do I pray for people who are sick? — 81
- Day 1: Be whole — 83
- Day 2: Be supported — 87

Day 3: Be careful	91
Day 4: Be quiet	97
Day 5: Be humble	101
Day 6: Be cleansed	107
Day 7: Reflection	111
Week 3: Group discussion questions	113
Week 4: What else do I need to think about?	115
Day 1: Be rested	117
Day 2: Be persistent	121
Day 3: Be thankful	125
Day 4: Be lovely	129
Day 5: Be mentored	133
Day 6: Be integrated	137
Day 7: Reflection	141
Week 4: Group discussion questions	143

Part 2: Organisational Context

Week 5: What is the role of the sacraments and other church traditions in healing and wholeness?	147
Day 1: Sacraments in healing – why bother?	149
Day 2: Initiating into wholeness: baptism and confirmation	153
Day 3: Sustaining wholeness: Holy Communion	157
Day 4: Restoring wholeness: reconciliation and anointing of the sick	161
Day 5: Other sacraments	165
Day 6: Reasons why people aren't physically healed	169

Day 7: Reflection 175
Week 5: Group discussion questions 177

Week 6: What else does my church/organisation need to consider? 179
    Day 1: Healing and wholeness within the church context 181
    Day 2: Consent, confidentiality and safeguarding 185
    Day 3: Managing risk 189
    Day 4: Oversight, governance, training and accountability 193
    Day 5: Group preparation 197
    Day 6: Sharing answers to prayer 201
    Day 7: Reflection 205
    Week 6: Group discussion questions 207

Part 3: Appendices
    Appendix A: A note to those in the healing professions 211
    Appendix B: Sermon suggestions 215
    Appendix C: Types of healing 221
    Appendix D: Glossary of spiritual gifts 223

Further reading 225
Acknowledgements 229
Bibliography 231

Part 1

Learning and Praying

Week 1

Does God care?

In a world where there is so much suffering and sickness, the first question we need to ask is, does God really care?

In this week we will begin to look at some big issues which we will unpack more, and from different perspectives, in the following weeks.

Day 1: The foot of the cross

"For God was pleased to have all his fullness dwell in him, and through him to reconcile to himself all things, whether things on earth or things in heaven, by making peace through his blood, shed on the cross."
Colossians 1:19-20

Every time we pray for healing and wholeness, we need to start by placing ourselves at the foot of the cross of Jesus. It is here, as we look up and see Jesus hanging on the cross, that we can begin to engage in the issues of pain, suffering and death.

Jesus, the Son of the invisible God, is the person in whom all things were created. All things were created in him and for him. It is in Jesus that all things hold together. It is therefore only through him, his death, his blood shed on the cross, that all things can be put back together. This, then, is the place to come when we recognise and seek our need to be made whole again, where broken things can be mended.

Does he really love us though? We may go through times in our lives when we feel abandoned by God and forgotten by him. We may be left feeling quite unloved. Maybe there are times when you have felt angry with God because of his apparent silence in the face of yours or someone else's suffering and pain. Psalm 13:1-2 says, "How long, Lord? Will you forget me for ever? How long will you hide your face from me? How long must I wrestle with my thoughts and day after day have sorrow in my heart?" Psalm 22:2 states, "My God, I cry out by day, but you do not answer, by night, but I find no rest." There may have been times when you have felt like this too. Job had a similar experience. In Job 19:7 he says, "Though I cry, 'Violence!' I get no response; though I call for help, there is no justice." Sometimes we can feel quite alone in our troubles and this is a normal part of Christian experience.

Jesus also understands. In Matthew 27, whilst on the cross, he cried out "My God, my God, why have you forsaken me?" (v.46). This is a quote from Psalm 22.

The good news is that, however we may feel at the time, God never abandons us. Deuteronomy 31:8 says, "The Lord himself goes before you and will be with you; he will never leave you nor forsake you." In Matthew 28:20, the risen Jesus says to his disciples, "And surely I am with you always, to the very end of the age."

Isaiah 53 is a passage which foretells the suffering of the coming Messiah. In it, we are told that Jesus was "despised and rejected by mankind, a man of suffering, and familiar with pain" (v.3). The passage goes on to say, "Surely he took up our pain and bore our suffering." Why would Jesus do this for us? The answer is, quite simply,

Day 1: The foot of the cross

because we have a God who loves us more than we can imagine. It is in his love and because of his compassion that we can ask for healing and wholeness.

But what do we mean by healing? We need healing from our brokenness in every sense. We tend to think about physical healing, but there are other sorts of healing which may be just as or even more important. We may need healing from the past, from memories, from abuse, from poor relationships, from difficult times we've been through, from emotional, spiritual or mental as well as physical pain. Fundamentally, we need to be brought back into a full relationship with our heavenly Father who made us and loves us. It is in his arms and by his strength and power that we can be made completely whole.

The famous passage in John 3:16 states, "For God so loved the world that he gave his one and only Son, that whoever believes in him shall not perish but have eternal life." It is here, at the foot of the cross, looking up at our Jesus who sacrificed himself for us, that we find ultimate love, ultimate compassion and ultimate power through his death.

> "I try to picture again the scene on Calvary, keeping my attention on the Central figure, until for me, Christ and Christ alone is in the picture. I then place myself at the foot of the cross, or, if you prefer it, I join the group already there of those who loved Him most."
>
> Edgar Bell

Exercise:

Close your eyes. If you can, spend some time imagining the scene with Jesus hanging on the cross. See his hands. See the nails. See his feet. See the crown of thorns.

You may find it helpful to sketch the scene. You don't need artistic talent – it's about focusing your mind on God who loves you and Jesus who died for you. Sketch yourself sitting at the foot of the cross. Alternatively, look at artwork which depicts the scene and imagine yourself in it.

Spend time just sitting quietly at the foot of the cross. Settle into this position – there, at the foot of the cross. Feel God's compassion and power wrap around you. Bring to him the past hurts, the losses, the anger, the pain – all the things you have locked away – start unlocking those boxes and taking out the things that hurt and showing them to God one by one. Tell God about them. He knows already but tell him anyway. Then know how much you are loved. If you don't feel loved, ask him to help you to feel and know his compassion and care for you. You have a loving God who cares deeply for you.

Each day, practise taking yourself to the foot of the cross of Jesus in this way. It takes a little practice so keep going!

Day 2: The God who forgives

"Jesus said, 'Father, forgive them, for they do not know what they are doing.'"
Luke 23:34

Central to our Christian faith is the understanding that Jesus died so that we can be forgiven. In 1 Corinthians 15:3-4, Paul writes, "For what I received I passed on to you as of first importance: that Christ died for our sins according to the Scriptures, that he was buried, that he was raised on the third day." It is because of our sin that Christ died. Even on the cross, as he hung for our sin, he was asking forgiveness for those who put him there. That includes us. He intercedes for us even as we pray. Hebrews 7:25 reassures us that Jesus "is able to save completely those who come to God through him, because he always lives to intercede for them".

You may feel that you have already received forgiveness from God in the past. This is great news. Psalm 103 reassures us that God has removed the dirty sinful bits of our lives as far away as east is from the west. Unfortunately, a bit like drinking water, we need to do this regularly. The odd drink of water once a week or less will not sustain your physical needs. Sin is part of being human and we need to ask regularly for forgiveness to sustain our spiritual needs. It is important to note that we are not always aware of when we have done wrong or failed to do right and so we need God's mercy to wipe away the unseen sin as well as what we know about.

The verses in Romans 7 apply to us all: "So I find this law at work: although I want to do good, evil is right there with me. For in my inner being I delight in God's law; but I see another law at work in me, waging war against the law of my mind and making me a prisoner of the law of sin at work within me. What a wretched man I am! Who will rescue me from this body that is subject to death? Thanks be to God, who delivers me through Jesus Christ our Lord! So then, I myself in my mind am a slave to God's law, but in my sinful nature a slave to the law of sin" (v.21-25). It is this daily need for spiritual cleansing that we need to take on board and put into practice as part of our own journey in sustaining wholeness.

How does this relate to Christian healing? The passage we looked at in Isaiah 53 yesterday shows us that it is because Jesus died for our sin that we can approach God for healing. It also says, "But he was pierced for our transgressions, he was crushed for our iniquities; the punishment that brought us peace was on him, and by his wounds we are healed" (v.5). It is Jesus' suffering, his wounds, his pain, the punishment he took onto himself for our sin which was meant for us – it is only by this that we can be forgiven and be made whole. This is how we can receive healing.

Day 2: The God who forgives

The problem is that being human, we are all naturally sinful. We need constant, repeated cleansing and forgiveness to maintain a good relationship with God. The good news is that forgiveness is available to anyone at any time of day or night. You do not need broadband or internet access. You do not have to wait in a call queue or find that the opening times for forgiveness are only between 09:00 and 09:05 on alternate Thursdays. It is available any time, anywhere, any day and to anyone!

Romans 5:6-11 puts it like this: "You see, at just the right time, when we were still powerless, Christ died for the ungodly. Very rarely will anyone die for a righteous person, though for a good person someone might possibly dare to die. But God demonstrates his own love for us in this: while we were still sinners, Christ died for us. Since we have now been justified by his blood, how much more shall we be saved from God's wrath through him! For if, while we were God's enemies, we were reconciled to him through the death of his Son, how much more, having been reconciled, shall we be saved through his life! Not only is this so, but we also boast in God through our Lord Jesus Christ, through whom we have now received reconciliation." Our salvation and our healing come through Jesus and through reconciliation to God.

The cross of Jesus is fundamentally about repentance and forgiveness. We need to acknowledge, confess and ask for forgiveness for ourselves, and then we need to forgive, or ask for help to forgive, those who have wronged us. By asking and accepting forgiveness, we can access part of the healing and wholeness that we need most. Coming into a right relationship with God is one of the most important aspects of healing that we seek. Healing and wholeness are therefore firstly and most importantly about redemption. Redemption is a word used in the slave trade which described the purchase or ransom by which the slave could be set free. It's used in the Bible to describe the action of being saved or saving from sin, error, or evil. This is what has been accomplished through the death of our loving Jesus on the cross.

> "I have ventured to call the healing wrought by the Church 'Redemptive Healing'. It is concerned with the making whole of persons, and not only with the patching up of sick or defective bodies or minds."
>
> Edgar Bell

Exercise:

Close your eyes. Imagine again the cross of Jesus. See him hanging there. Find your seat again at the foot of the cross, perhaps looking up to him. Bring to him the wrong things that you have done or the right things that you have not done and all the things we don't even know about. Perhaps things from the distant past as well as the last few days. Hear him ask his Father for forgiveness for you – "Father, forgive them" applies to us all. Know that as you bring these to him, they vanish into thin air. Spend a little more time sitting at the foot of the cross, knowing you are loved, cherished and forgiven.

Day 3: The God who gives

> "Which of you, if your son asks for bread, will give him a stone? Or if he asks for a fish, will give him a snake? If you, then, though you are evil, know how to give good gifts to your children, how much more will your Father in heaven give good gifts to those who ask him!"
> Matthew 7:9-11

Not only has God given us Jesus, the chance for forgiveness, for reconciliation to him and, ultimately, eternal life, he is a God who loves to give us good things. He also cares about the smaller things in life. It is well worth remembering that Jesus' first miracle was the turning of water into wine at a party. We are so blessed to be in relationship with a God like this!

In Romans 8:32 we are told, "He who did not spare his own Son, but gave him up for us all – how will he not also, along with him, graciously give us all things?" We follow and worship a God of infinite generosity.

We are also encouraged to ask God for things. John 16:24 encourages us to "ask and you will receive", although, of course, this is almost certainly in the context of spiritual blessings and the coming of the kingdom of God rather than a holiday home in Tenerife.

Over the last two days we have brought things to God that we need to get rid of – pain from the past, anger and hurt on Day 1 and sin on Day 2. Today we need to think about what we need to receive to be "in tune" with God when we start asking for healing and wholeness of others. What do we need to be asking him for?

The answer is that we really need the Holy Spirit and everything that he (or she) brings. It is through the presence and the power mediated by the Holy Spirit that healing occurs. The Holy Spirit is a gift for us, promised and given by God (Acts 1). We rely completely on the power and guidance of the Holy Spirit when we pray for healing and wholeness for others. We don't always know what we are praying for. For example, someone may have come to us wanting prayer for a sore knee and then we find that God is more interested in healing them from the pain of being abandoned as a child . . . or something like that. They may or may not get the knee healed as well. We cannot know these things ourselves, so we become totally reliant on the Spirit. The "Spirit searches all things, even the deep things of God" (1 Corinthians 2:10) and therefore knows and understands the brokenness and where and how healing prayer is needed. Furthermore, in Romans 8:26 we are reassured that "the Spirit helps us in our weakness. We do not know what we ought to pray for, but the Spirit himself intercedes for us through wordless groans".

The Holy Spirit is also our advocate, and the advocate for those that we pray for. It is through him (or her – note the original noun is feminine) that we will be taught the things of God, and that we will receive peace (John 14). Deep peace amid the turmoil of suffering, illness and pain, is invaluable.

You may feel that you have already asked for and been filled with the Holy Spirit. However, asking for the Spirit is a bit like asking for forgiveness. We cannot ever ask enough for forgiveness and, in the same way, we can never ask enough to be more filled by the Spirit. We aren't like cars getting fuelled – the tank doesn't get to a point it's full and you cannot have any more until you've used some of what you have. You worship and are loved by a generous God – just ask!

Exercise:

Close your eyes. Sit quietly. Take some slow, deep breaths. Ask your heavenly Father to fill you with his Holy Spirit, to open your spiritual eyes and ears and prepare you for praying for others. Ask to be filled with the fruits and the gifts that you need for the job ahead.

Day 4: Suffering

"You've kept track of my every toss and turn through the sleepless nights, each tear entered in your ledger, each ache written in your book."

Psalm 56:8 (The Message)[1]

So, here we are – Day 4 – and we are going to tackle the most sticky of sticky issues in healing and wholeness – suffering. But let me just be clear. In the next 20 minutes, we are not all going to become expert theologians on the complexities of the issues of suffering. Apart from anything else, nobody fully understands this and we are going to have to, at least in part, accept the uncertainty around it. The question I seek to address today is: what do we need to understand to be able to do the job that we are asked to do – that is, pray for and with others for healing?

Cups of tea at the ready? Let's go!

Firstly, when God originally created the world in which we live, it was good (Genesis 1). Now, look on your preferred news website. See the articles about wars,

---

1. *The Message*, copyright © 1993, 2002, 2018 by Eugene H. Peterson. Used by permission of NavPress. All rights reserved. Represented by Tyndale House Publishers, Inc.

famines, earthquakes, etc. Is this world we live in still good? No. Clearly something has gone badly wrong. What went wrong is recounted in Genesis chapter 3. Because of the sin and disobedience of Adam and Eve, we became sinful people living in a sinful and cursed world. In fact, in Romans 8:21 we are told that the earth is in "bondage to decay". In some ways, then, the ship that we are on is sinking.

Because of Jesus' death on the cross, we can overcome some of the bad effects of Genesis 3. We have free access to forgiveness any time of the day or night. God's forgiveness freely restores us in our faithful walk with our loving heavenly Father. But, we cannot undo the impact human disobedience had on the world in which we live. We are told that creation has "been groaning as in the pains of childbirth right up to the present time" (Romans 8:22). The creation is also looking forward to its own liberation and renewal . . . but it hasn't happened yet. Natural disasters are one symptom of the world suffering from the curse it is under.

Secondly, for reasons that aren't clear, it appears that Satan has some authority in the world. We will explore this a little further next week when we think about spiritual battles, but for now I would suggest you have a look at Luke 4, which is the story of the temptations of Jesus. In the second temptation, the devil shows Jesus all the kingdoms of the world and says to him, "I will give you all their authority and splendour; it has been given to me, and I can give it to anyone I want to" (v.6). Satan couldn't offer to give something to Jesus which wasn't his in the first place.

Finally, there is the thinking that alleviation from suffering is not part of the new covenant. The old covenant, given through Moses, was the law. It included things like sacrificing lambs for sin. In the new covenant, this is replaced by Jesus' death and resurrection – we have a new contract with God. We no longer have to sacrifice lambs, Jesus has sacrificed himself for us – the ultimate and last sacrificial lamb.

It's a bit like getting a new mobile phone contract. There are things which you may have unlimited access to – local calls and text messages, for example. But there are also things that are not in the contract – calls to and from abroad, for example. In the new covenant, we have free and instant access to forgiveness from sin and relationship with God. Anytime, anywhere, anyone. We have free and instant access to Jesus and help and advocacy from our mentor, the Holy Spirit. That's all part of the contract. But instant immediate access to physical healing is not. That doesn't mean it cannot and doesn't happen, it just means that we don't seem to have an automatic entitlement to it.

The good news is that this broken condition that we and the world are in now is temporary. There will be a time in the future where there will be a new heaven and a new earth. All suffering and conflict will be gone. There will be no crying and no tears. But, we aren't there yet, and the creation is still groaning.

I hope this goes some way to making it easier to understand why sickness and natural disaster happen. However, I must be honest – none of the above has helped me feel any better when faced with a situation of pain, suffering or untimely death. What has helped is a powerful spiritual experience I had when I was a teenager. I got very angry with God about an issue of suffering and God, in return, showed me very powerfully that he was much more upset than I was. It is as if my ability to show love and compassion is a tiny drop compared with the ocean of God's emotions. In the same way, my angry, frustrated tears are also tiny compared with his. In John 11, when Jesus goes to the tomb of his friend Lazarus who had died, he wept. We are told he was "deeply moved" (v.33). He wept so much that everyone around him said, "See how he loved him!" (v.36). This has brought me enormous comfort and helped me to keep going when things are bad.

Exercise:

Reflect back on your difficult times. Thank God that, whatever the reasons why suffering happens, he cares deeply about it and he cares deeply about you. It's worth noting that an alternative translation for our verse today is that God collects our tears in a bottle.

Day 5: Why pray for the sick?

"When Jesus had called the Twelve together, he gave them power and authority to drive out all demons and to cure diseases, and he sent them out to proclaim the kingdom of God and to heal those who were ill."
Luke 9:1-2

Praying for the sick was part of the ministry of Jesus. When he started his ministry and read from the scroll in Nazareth (which foretells the coming of the Messiah), he proclaimed that his ministry was to include release of captives, healing of the blind and setting free of the oppressed (Luke 4:18-19). He starts to fulfil it immediately with the healing of many (Luke 4:40). When John the Baptist was in prison, he seems to have had some doubts about whether Jesus really was who he thought and so sent his disciples to ask Jesus for some reassurance. Jesus responds by saying, "Go back and report to John what you hear and see: the blind receive sight, the lame walk, those who have leprosy are cleansed, the deaf hear, the dead are raised, and the good news is proclaimed to the poor" (Matthew 11:4-5).

When Jesus sent out his twelve disciples he "gave them authority to drive out impure spirits and to heal every disease and illness" (Matthew 10:1). They were told to "proclaim this message: 'The kingdom of heaven has come near.' Heal those who are ill, raise the dead, cleanse those who have leprosy, drive out demons. Freely you have received; freely give" (Matthew 10:7-8). So the first reason we pray for the sick is because we have received freely and we have to give freely. We have been told to give generously in the same way God has generously given to us.

We may feel that we are not as special as the twelve disciples. We are just ordinary people trying to do right and good things with our lives for the benefit of others. But later on, he sends out seventy-two others (ordinary people like you and me) with the instructions to "heal those there who are ill and tell them, 'The kingdom of God has come near to you'" (Luke 10:8-9). So the second reason that we pray for the sick is because we have been commanded to do so.

Furthermore, Jesus said that anyone who believed in him would be able to "place their hands on people who are ill, and they will get well" (Mark 16:18). Note the need to place hands on the sick – we need to be praying with people, not just for them. In addition, in John's gospel, it says, "Very truly I tell you, whoever believes in me will do the works I have been doing, and they will do even greater things than these, because I am going to the Father" (John 14:12). Again, note this applies to anyone who believes in Jesus. That includes me and you.

Day 5: Why pray for the sick?

Jesus has shared his power with us and we are commanded to go and use it for the benefit of others. I would suggest that we are meant to be obedient regardless of how we feel about it. But we need to trust the outcome of our obedience to God. We are not responsible for the results when we pray for healing – we will work through this more in Week 3 and Week 4.

It is also worth noting that Jesus never refused someone who asked him for healing. Therefore, if someone asks us to pray for their healing, we are meant to say yes.

However, without doubt, there are some people who are given a particular spiritual gift for healing (1 Corinthians 12). But we are all called to engage in this activity, regardless of whether we feel particularly gifted in it or not. You may not find out whether you have this as a gift or are able to develop your gifting in this area if you don't start trying.

In his book *The Practice of Healing Prayer*, Francis MacNutt suggests that people have lost faith in healing prayer in three ways. Firstly, we don't expect healing to happen when we pray. Secondly, we have lost the confidence that anyone can pray. Thirdly, that when we do pray, it is at a distance. We need to be praying with the laying on of hands.

Prayer for healing with the laying on of hands needs to be an ordinary, normal part of everyone's Christian life, not something exceptional or extraordinary.

At the Foot of the Cross

"We should have expectant faith that, regardless of how it happens, great good comes out of our prayers. I have seen so many wonderful things take place that I believe it is a sad mistake not to pray whenever we have the chance. We have everything to gain, with little to lose."

Francis MacNutt[2]

> ## Exercise:
>
> Spend time today at the foot of the cross waiting on the Holy Spirit and asking to be filled with the confidence and courage to pray for others. Then ask for the gifts you need to perform the task – compassion, listening, praying, discernment – as well as spiritual gifts of healing and wholeness.

---

2. Francis MacNutt, *The Practice of Healing Prayer* (Word Among Us Press, 2010), p.95.

Day 6: The power of the resurrection

"But Christ has indeed been raised from the dead, the firstfruits of those who have fallen asleep. For since death came through a man, the resurrection of the dead comes also through a man. For as in Adam all die, so in Christ all will be made alive."
1 Corinthians 15:20-22

We started this week with reflecting on the cross, the place of pain and suffering but also the place of ultimate power, ultimate love and ultimate compassion. We finish this week with thinking about the power of the resurrection, which demonstrates the defeat of the devil, of death, suffering and sickness. It is through the resurrection of Jesus that the suffering on the cross and death itself is fully overcome.

Jesus himself stated, "I am the resurrection and the life. The one who believes in me will live, even though they die; and whoever lives by believing in me will never die" (John 11:25-26). Therefore, there is not just healing and wholeness here, there is an avoidance of death altogether.

Christ did not only rise from the dead, he ascended into heaven and sits at the right hand of God. The verse we looked at yesterday from John 14 where Jesus says that we will do even greater things, ends with the words "because I am going to the Father" (v.12). It is because Jesus is now seated at the right hand of God that we can ask for healing and wholeness.

Although I usually imagine bringing whoever I am praying for to the foot of the cross of Jesus for healing and wholeness, I sometimes imagine bringing them to the throne room of God instead. So what do we know about the throne room?

We know that it is the place that Jesus went to after his ascension and where he sits at the right hand of God the Father because of having endured the cross. Hebrews 12:2 says, "For the joy that was set before him he endured the cross, scorning its shame, and sat down at the right hand of the throne of God."

We know it is the place where justice and righteousness are established forever and over all things. Hebrews 1:8 says, "But about the Son he says, 'Your throne, O God, will last for ever and ever; a sceptre of justice will be the sceptre of your kingdom." Isaiah 9:7 predicts, "Of the greatness of his government and peace there will be no end. He will reign on David's throne and over his kingdom, establishing and upholding it with justice and righteousness from that time on and for ever." Psalm 103:19 states, "The Lord has established his throne in heaven, and his kingdom rules over all."

Secondly, it is the focus of praise and worship of God. Revelation 5:13 says, "Then I heard every creature in heaven and on earth and under the earth and on the sea, and all that is in them, saying: 'To him who sits on the throne and to the Lamb be praise and honour and glory and power, for ever and ever!'"

Thirdly, there is a river that flows from the throne which is life-giving and healing. In Revelation 22:1-3 we are told, "Then the angel showed me the river of the water of life, as clear as crystal, flowing from the throne of God and of the Lamb down the middle of the great street of the city. On each side of the river stood the tree of life, bearing twelve crops of fruit, yielding its fruit every month. And the leaves of the tree are for the healing of the nations. No longer will there be any curse."

Finally, we are told to approach the throne with confidence because it is also the centre for grace and mercy when we are in need. Hebrews 4:14-16 states, "Therefore, since we have a great high priest who has ascended into heaven, Jesus the Son of God, let us hold firmly to the faith we profess. For we do not have a high priest who is unable to feel sympathy for our weaknesses, but we have one who has been tempted in every way, just as we are – yet he did not sin. Let us then approach God's throne of grace with confidence, so that we may receive mercy and find grace to help us in our time of need."

Therefore, when you bring someone to Jesus in healing prayer, you may find there are times when you picture bringing them to the throne room of God instead of the foot of the cross. Here there is power, judgment and a place of holiness. But there is also grace, mercy and it is the source of the river of life.

"Here we are brought into contact with the Redemptive process in its fulness. We are borne along from the Manger Throne to worship at the Throne of the Ascended Christ."

Edgar Bell

Exercise:

This time, instead of picturing the foot of the cross of Christ, spend some time picturing the throne room of God. It's much harder to do as we don't really know quite what it looks like. Again, feel the presence of the power of God here, his love, his grace, his mercy.

Day 7: Reflection

It's time to rest, relax and reflect.

> "The LORD reigns, let the earth be glad;
> let the distant shores rejoice.
> Clouds and thick darkness surround him;
> righteousness and justice are the foundation of
> his throne.
> Fire goes before him
> and consumes his foes on every side.
> His lightning lights up the world;
> the earth sees and trembles.
> The mountains melt like wax before the LORD,
> before the LORD of all the earth.
> The heavens proclaim his righteousness,
> and all peoples see his glory."
>
> (Psalm 97:1-6)

Find something of God's creation and thank him for it. It doesn't have to be a mountain – an indoor pot plant will do. Or watch the birds or flowers or trees that you can see from the window. Thank God for his power as well as his care.

Week 1: Group discussion questions

The list of questions below are suggestions only. The group may have other areas they wish to explore. Encourage group members to discuss and reflect on their experiences.

1. How have you found this week? Was there anything that surprised or struck you? Was there anything new or different? Is there anything that you didn't understand or disagreed with?
2. What do you think is the difference between healing and wholeness? Which do you think is more important to God?
3. There are different types of healing (see Appendix C). Can you think of examples in the Bible or within your own experience of each? Do we always know what type of healing is required when we pray for someone?
4. Read Psalm 22:1-5. Notice the sense of abandonment by God during times of difficulty. What encouragement can we find in this psalm to get us through these times?
5. How do you think the idea of redemption relates to healing and wholeness? Why is this important?

6. Read Matthew 7:7-12. The passage shows what a generous God we have. How do you begin to reconcile a generous God who loves to give with times when we don't see him provide the healing that we are asking for?

7. Before raising Lazarus from the dead, Jesus wept and was deeply moved. How do you think God feels about situations of suffering and illness that we bring to him?

8. In his book *The Practice of Healing Prayer*, Francis MacNutt suggests that people have lost faith in healing prayer in three ways. Firstly, we don't expect healing to happen when we pray. Secondly, we have lost the confidence that anyone can pray. Thirdly, that when we do pray, it is at a distance. To what extent do you think this is true for you? How about your church/organisation?

9. The throne room of God is a place of mercy, grace and life. It is also a place of worship. Do you think that there is a link between worship and healing? If so, what is it?

As a group you could try this as an exercise. Using a picture or pictures of Jesus on the cross, and some music in the background, encourage the group to spend some time quietly imagining taking themselves to the foot of the cross of Jesus.

Week 2:

Why don't we always see physical healing?

In Week 1 we saw that we have a God who loves us. We found the foot of the cross as the place to seek healing. We learnt that we engage with the issues of suffering, pain and death through the cross of Jesus. But we also learnt that forgiveness is a central part of all of this. We looked a bit at the issues around suffering and learnt that, however little we understand it, we have a God who cares deeply for us. We found him to be a God who weeps and is moved by situations. We found him to be a generous God. Finally, we reflected on his throne of power and grace as an alternative healing venue.

This week the focus will switch from ourselves and our needs, to God and who he is. A better understanding of his character, perspective and ways will help us to understand how we pray for healing and wholeness for others. We seek to better understand how a loving God doesn't always grant us the physical healing we ask for.

Day 1: God's priorities

> "'Which is easier: to say to this paralysed man, "Your sins are forgiven," or to say, "Get up, take your mat and walk"? But I want you to know that the Son of Man has authority on earth to forgive sins.' So he said to the man, 'I tell you, get up, take your mat and go home.'"
>
> Mark 2:9-11

In this story, Jesus is preaching in a crowded room that was so full, it had overflowed and there was no room even outside of the door. Four friends dug through the roof of the room he was in and lowered their paralysed friend on his mat through it. When Jesus saw their faith, he said to the paralysed man, "Son, your sins are forgiven" (v.5). The story almost appears to stop there with the main points being: the faith of the four friends and the lengths they have gone to show this; the calling of the paralysed man "son"; and the forgiveness of his sins. Presumably, the friends hadn't lowered him through the roof because they thought he had sins that needed forgiving – we assume that they lowered him down because they wanted to see his physical healing.

We are left wondering whether, if there hadn't been teachers of the law present getting angry with Jesus for forgiving sin, would this man have received the physical healing he and his friends sought? As it was, the man receives full physical healing because of the need to demonstrate that Jesus could forgive sin.

There are two things here. Firstly, Jesus really needed people to understand that he can forgive sin. This is presumably much harder to achieve (as it is the remit of God alone) but also much harder to demonstrate than physical healing. Unlimited access to forgiveness of our sins, as we have already seen, was the central part of the new covenant. Secondly, that Jesus' priority here seems to be forgiveness of sin – wholeness rather than physical healing. This is not usually our priority when we pray for people, usually because we don't know or understand what is required for someone to be made whole. We are reliant, as always, on the power and direction of the Holy Spirit in our prayers.

There are other accounts in the gospels where the forgiveness of sin appears to be an important part of physical healing, but there are also numerous accounts when it isn't. We learn that God appears to prioritise wholeness over just physical healing, but often physical healing is a part of this. Hence, we may be made whole in areas which are of most importance without being fully physically restored.

The other issue around forgiveness in healing is the need to forgive others. Sometimes our unforgiveness and bitterness towards others who have wronged us

Day 1: God's priorities

is an important part of the healing and wholeness that we seek. Forgiveness of others is a pre-requisite for our own forgiveness. Matthew 6:14-15 states, "For if you forgive other people when they sin against you, your heavenly Father will also forgive you. But if you do not forgive others their sins, your Father will not forgive your sins." We also have to do this repeatedly – seventy-seven times (Matthew 18:21-22)!

So, our need to forgive others and our own need for forgiveness seem to be a priority for God over and above physical healing. It is not, usually, our priority.

The next thing is that when people are physically healed it is for a purpose. In the story of the man born blind in John 9, we are told, "His disciples asked him, 'Rabbi, who sinned, this man or his parents, that he was born blind?' 'Neither this man nor his parents sinned,' said Jesus, 'but this happened so that the works of God might be displayed in him'" (v.2-3). Here, the purpose of healing is so that the works of God can be displayed in him – it is to give glory to God.

In other stories, the results of healing are to bring people into God's service. At the start of Luke 8 we are told of a number of women who were cured from diseases who devoted themselves to God's service as a result. The same is true of the healing of Legion later on in the same chapter. This suggests that the primary purpose of healing and wholeness is for the glory of God and to bring people into his service. It is not to allow us to go back to our lives as they were before our sickness, but to transform our lives so that we can follow Jesus even more closely.

In the healing of Hezekiah (in 2 Kings 20), Hezekiah's years of devotion and service appear to be a prerequisite for his healing. Similarly, in Isaiah 58, the fact that "your healing will quickly appear" (v.8) is in response to service to the poor, the oppressed and those suffering injustice. In these examples, it would appear that sometimes service results in healing rather than the other way round.

> "Our Lord is not concerned primarily with the mere restoration of sick persons to a state of physical health ... Christian healing should always be to the Glory of God and never to the Glory of the one ministering healing. Christian healing should always be for service. A person so restored is not restored merely to be physically or mentally well, but for the service of Christ."
>
> Edgar Bell

Exercise:

Read through the different types of healing listed in Appendix 3. Which ones do you think God prioritises and which do we pray for? Have there been times that God has made you more whole through healing in one of these areas? How has it led you further into his service? Thank him for these times.

Day 2: God's kingdom

> "When you enter a town and are welcomed, eat what is offered to you. Heal those there who are ill and tell them, 'The kingdom of God has come near to you.'"
>
> Luke 10:8-9

Healing the sick is part of the demonstration of the kingdom of God. So what is the kingdom of God and what do we need to understand about it in order to do the job we have been asked to do – that is to pray and lay hands on the sick?

The prophet Daniel foretold (amongst others) that there would be a kingdom of God established during the days of the Roman Empire and through David's descendants (Daniel 2:44). When Jesus stood up in Nazareth in Luke 4 and read from a passage telling of the coming Messiah and promised King, he stated it was being fulfilled that day. Jesus was, in fact, claiming the start of the new kingdom of God.

However, the kingdom of God is close to us but not yet fully here. Most commentators agree that we are living in a time of the "now and not yet". We see glimpses of the kingdom through, for example, the occasional miraculous sign and with the demonstration of the gifts of the Holy Spirit. But it isn't fully here yet.

Revelation 21:4 gives us an idea of the sort of place the world will be when the kingdom of God is here in full. It says, "He will wipe every tear from their eyes. There will be no more death or mourning or crying or pain, for the old order of things has passed away." Isaiah 11, which predicts the coming of a Messiah, also gives us some idea of this new order. This includes, "The infant will play near the cobra's den, and the young child will put its hand into the viper's nest. They will neither harm nor destroy" (v.8-9).

Jesus' ministry was a demonstration of this new kingdom. But even Jesus was not always able to do the miracles he wanted. In Mark 6, when Jesus visited his hometown, we are told, "He could not do any miracles there" (v.5). This was probably because of a lack of faith in Jesus and who he was. Furthermore, although Jesus was filled with the Spirit all the time, there were times when the Spirit came on Jesus with particular power. For example, we are told in Luke 5:17 that "the power of the Lord was with Jesus to heal those who were ill", which suggests that maybe there were other times when this wasn't the case.

It is also worth remembering that Jesus urged us to pray regularly for the kingdom of God to come. The Lord's Prayer includes the lines "your kingdom come, your will be done, on earth as it is in heaven" (Matthew 6:10). This suggests that the kingdom isn't here fully yet and that God's will is not always done.

All in all, from our point of view as ordinary people trying to understand prayer for healing, it means the following: firstly, if there were times and places Jesus couldn't do miracles, then we shouldn't be expecting too much of ourselves. Secondly, that the Holy Spirit is unpredictable. There appear to be times and places when he is uniquely present and powerful and those when he is not. Thirdly, that as we live in a time of the now and not yet of the kingdom of God, we will sometimes see and hear of amazing things that happen, but there will also be times when we don't. Fourthly, that we need to pray earnestly for the kingdom of God to come so we see more of God's powerful work.

Finally, is the issue of God's will. There are some healing commentators who argue that it is always God's will to heal and that we should never pray "if it is your will" when we pray for someone else to be healed. They argue that this is a cop out for us. I think, on balance, I would agree. If the Lord's Prayer says that we should be praying that God's will to be done, we have to assume that much of the time it is not. I think it is worth noting that Jesus prayed, "Father, if you are willing, take this cup from me; yet not my will, but yours be done" (Luke 22:42) just before his arrest. So we need to pray that God's kingdom comes and his will is done when we pray for healing and wholeness.

> ### Exercise:
> Spend some time today praying for God's kingdom to come in power. Then spend some time praying for God's will to be done.

Day 3: God's methods

> "In the thirty-ninth year of his reign Asa was afflicted with a disease in his feet. Though his disease was severe, even in his illness he did not seek help from the LORD, but only from the doctors."
>
> 2 Chronicles 16:12

Today we are going to look a little at the processes and methods God uses to heal. Throughout the Old Testament, we are told of kings who did evil in the eyes of the Lord and those who were good guys. King Asa was one of the good guys. He was passionate about reforming the nation, bringing it back to God and getting rid of idolatry. However, despite his desire to return people back to God, we are told that as he got older, he developed a disease of the feet. God appears to have been annoyed that he did not seek help from him for this but only medical help.

I don't think that the Bible is suggesting that we should either pray or seek medical help. Rather that we should be doing both. There is some suggestion in more recent healing literature that they can work synergistically

– for example, prayer enhancing the effects of the medical treatment. So, the first thing to say about God's methods is that often he uses medicine and doctors to heal. God has put healing into the natural processes of our bodies, and consequently most people get better most of the time. Modern medicine seeks to understand how this happens, and consequently works along with God's innate healing.

Secondly, healing is usually a process requiring a lot of prayer over a long period of time. God often heals gradually. The instantaneous complete healing, although it does happen, is much rarer than the gradual healing occurring over time. Even with Jesus, healing wasn't always instantaneous. In Mark 8:23-25 we read, "He took the blind man by the hand and led him outside the village. When he had spat on the man's eyes and put his hands on him, Jesus asked, 'Do you see anything?' He looked up and said, 'I see people; they look like trees walking around.' Once more Jesus put his hands on the man's eyes. Then his eyes were opened, his sight was restored, and he saw everything clearly." Jesus had to have two attempts for sight to be fully restored, so we may need a few hundred.

Thirdly, no two healings are ever the same. This is as true today as it was in the accounts in the Bible. Every healing, like every person, is unique and different. For example, if you look at the stories of healing of people who are blind, we have the story in Mark 8 with two attempts and the use of spit. We also have the Luke 18 story where Jesus simply says, "Receive your sight" (v.42), and it happens. Then we have the John 9 story of the man born blind when Jesus uses spit and mud, and then sends the man to wash in the Pool of Siloam.

Fourthly, Jesus asked whether people wanted to be healed. He didn't assume they did. He often asked them to articulate what they wanted God to do for them. For example, when he heals a man lying by the pool in John 5:5-6, we are told, "One who was there had been an invalid for thirty-eight years. When Jesus saw him lying there and learned that he had been in this condition for a long time, he asked him, 'Do you want to get well?'" In Mark 10:51 he asks blind Bartimaeus, "What do you want me to do for you?" We are told that "The blind man said, 'Rabbi, I want to see.'"

Finally, there is the role of faith. We will explore this more in Week 4, but for now just to note that faith in the power of a loving Jesus through his death on the cross is sometimes a pre-requisite for healing in the Bible. The good news is that we only need faith as small as a mustard seed (Matthew 17:20) for God to do great things!

Exercise:

Thank God that he deals with us all differently. Thank him that he takes an individual approach to our problems. Thank him for the gift of faith. Ask him to increase it in you.

Day 4: God's claim

"When you believed, you were marked in him with a seal, the promised Holy Spirit, who is a deposit guaranteeing our inheritance until the redemption of those who are God's possession – to the praise of his glory."
Ephesians 1:13-14

When we become Christians and believe in our God who loves us, we are marked with a seal which shows that we now belong to God's family. We become his possession and we get our spiritual inheritance from him. This is mediated by the Holy Spirit. In Revelation 7 and 9 we are told that the servants of God have a seal on their foreheads and the seal protects them from harm. We are told that Jesus had a seal of approval (John 6:27) and 2 Timothy 2:19 says, "Nevertheless, God's solid foundation stands firm, sealed with this inscription: 'The Lord knows those who are his,' and, 'Everyone who confesses the name of the Lord must turn away from wickedness.'"

This is, perhaps, analogous to the Exodus 12 passage which tells of the flight from Egypt of the Israelite nation. They were commanded to smear blood from a lamb on the door frames of their houses, which would mark them and so keep them safe from the destructive plague. In the same way, we are marked as being children of God and under his protection.

It isn't the only time we are told that we become children of God. For example, in John 1:12-13 we read, "Yet to all who did receive him, to those who believed in his name, he gave the right to become children of God – children born not of natural descent, nor of human decision or a husband's will, but born of God." Also, in 1 John 3:1 it says, "See what great love the Father has lavished on us, that we should be called children of God!"

In some of the stories of healing, Jesus refers to those being healed as "son" or "daughter". We have seen this in the story of the paralysed man being lowered through the roof by his friends who Jesus calls "son". In Luke 8 he calls the woman whom he heals from her bleeding "daughter". I wonder whether Jesus is bringing them into the family of God by doing this and whether this is part of the wholeness and healing they and we need?

In any case, we learn that when we become Christians, we are marked by God as his children. The marking guarantees our inheritance as well as our place in his family. God is protective of us. God has claimed us as his own.

This becomes really important when we pray for others to be healed and made whole. Often, when we bring others to God, we state our own claim on them. They are our friends or close family member, member of our fellowship, etc. They may even be people we've never met, but we really want God to do something specific for them. We bring them to God with our vision blurred by our own desires and wants for them. If they are family, we also claim them as our family and their importance to us.

The problem is this: if we are going to hand them over to God fully, leave them in his presence and power, sometimes the first thing we need to do is to relinquish our own claim. Relinquishing our claim sometimes needs to be a repetitive act of determination. We must give the person we pray for to God and ask him to claim them, whilst relinquishing our own claim on them.

We may also need to get rid of the noise and the fuss going on around the unwell person. In Luke 8, when Jesus arrives at Jairus' house because his daughter has died, we are told, "When he arrived at the house of Jairus, he did not let anyone go in with him except Peter, John and James, and the child's father and mother" (v.51). He removes all the mourners and those weeping and wailing from the scene. He just takes his three closest mentees and the parents. Everyone not in "the zone" is removed.

> "If [the person praying] is to be of any real use, he or she must be ready to eliminate all personal wishes in any particular case. Only God's will for the sufferer must be desired and sought and if revealed and recognised, should be welcomed and

accepted. It is therefore necessary to learn how to set aside all self-will and all personal wishes and desires, if intercession is to be so much more than wishful thinking."

Edgar Bell

Exercise:

Thank God that he has claimed you as his own. Ask for his help in letting go into his hands those that you love and pray for.

Day 5: God's enemies

"Do not be afraid, Daniel. Since the first day that you set your mind to gain understanding and to humble yourself before your God, your words were heard, and I have come in response to them. But the prince of the Persian kingdom resisted me twenty-one days. Then Michael, one of the chief princes, came to help me, because I was detained there with the king of Persia. Now I have come to explain to you what will happen to your people in the future, for the vision concerns a time yet to come."

Daniel 10:12-14

In this rather strange passage, Daniel's answer to prayer is delayed because of a spiritual battle. When the angel with the answer does appear, three weeks later, he gives an explanation for where he has been. Most commentators agree that the prince of Persia and king of Persia probably relate to high-ranking demons. The Archangel Michael is associated elsewhere in the Bible with leading the battle against the devil and his followers (see Jude 9 and Revelation 12). Daniel persisted in prayer and "mourning" for three weeks until the battle was won and he got the answer that he needed.

The devil is referred to as the Prince of this world and that the whole world is under his control (1 John 5:19). He is described as a thief who comes only to steal and kill and destroy (John 10:10). We are reassured that Jesus came to drive out the devil (John 12:31) and to destroy his work (1 John 3:8). The driving out of the devil's empire is a sign that the kingdom of God has come (Matthew 12:28). But, as we've already seen, we are in a time of the now and the not yet.

We have been given authority over the enemy through Jesus. After sending out the seventy-two in Luke 10, they came back to report to Jesus. We are told, "The seventy-two returned with joy and said, 'Lord, even the demons submit to us in your name.' He replied, 'I saw Satan fall like lightning from heaven. I have given you authority to trample on snakes and scorpions and to overcome all the power of the enemy; nothing will harm you. However, do not rejoice that the spirits submit to you, but rejoice that your names are written in heaven'" (v.17-20).

We are also protected from Satan by Jesus because we are children of God. 1 John 5:18-19 states, "We know that anyone born of God does not continue to sin; the One who was born of God keeps them safe, and the evil one cannot harm them. We know that we are children of God, and that the whole world is under the control of the evil one." Again, in 1 John 4:4 we are told, "You, dear children, are from God and have overcome them, because the one who is in you is greater than the one who is in the world."

However, we are warned not to become complacent. 1 Peter 5:8 tells us to "be alert and of sober mind. Your enemy the devil prowls around like a roaring lion looking for someone to devour". Ephesians 6:11-12 says, "Put on the full armour of God, so that you can take your stand against the devil's schemes. For our struggle is not against flesh and blood, but against the rulers, against the authorities, against the powers of this dark world and against the spiritual forces of evil in the heavenly realms."

But, until Jesus comes again, we continue to be in the middle of a spiritual battle. As John Wimber writes, "We are locked in spiritual warfare until Christ's return."[3] Ultimately, Satan will be defeated. We already have victory through the cross of Jesus and we are protected by him. Evil cannot harm us.

So what does this mean when we pray for someone? Very simply, we may be engaging in spiritual battles that we do not know and cannot see. We take the person we are praying for to one of the two places of real safety that the devil will not go – the foot of the cross of Jesus where Satan has been defeated, or into the throne room of our heavenly Father. You already know how to do this – we practised this last week. We

---

3. John Wimber and Kevin Springer, *Power Healing* (New York: HarperCollins, 1987).

bring whoever we are praying for to a place of safety. We then, like Daniel, need to pray persistently.

Finally, we are not alone when we pray for someone. We have the help, protection and mentoring of the Holy Spirit. Christ Jesus himself also intercedes for us.

Exercise:

Romans 8:34-39 says, "Who then is the one who condemns? No one. Christ Jesus who died – more than that, who was raised to life – is at the right hand of God and is also interceding for us. Who shall separate us from the love of Christ? Shall trouble or hardship or persecution or famine or nakedness or danger or sword? As it is written: 'For your sake we face death all day long; we are considered as sheep to be slaughtered.' No, in all these things we are more than conquerors through him who loved us. For I am convinced that neither death nor life, neither angels nor demons, neither the present nor the future, nor any powers, neither height nor depth, nor anything else in all creation, will be able to separate us from the love of God that is in Christ Jesus our Lord."

Spend time thanking God for his immense power and immense love and that nothing can separate us from him. Also thank him that he intercedes for us.

Day 6: God's perspective

"'For my thoughts are not your thoughts, neither are your ways my ways,' declares the LORD. 'As the heavens are higher than the earth, so are my ways higher than your ways and my thoughts than your thoughts.'"
Isaiah 55:8-9

I wonder whether sometimes we try and bring God down to our own size. He existed before time, exists outside of time, created time and the universe we live in, the things we can see and the things we cannot. Yet we expect to be able to understand what goes on and feel frustrated and angry if we don't. Ultimately, if we were to completely understand God, then surely, by definition, he could not be God. By implication, God's perspective is rarely the same as ours.

The book of Job is a story of suffering. The first thirty-seven chapters explore the story of Job. It explores whether he is suffering because of his sin (he is not) and other possible causes for the pain he is in. It is interesting that when God ultimately responds to Job, he does not give him any straight answers. Instead, he says, "Brace yourself like a man; I will question you, and you shall answer me. Where were you when I laid the earth's foundation? Tell me, if you understand. Who marked off its dimensions? Surely you know! Who stretched a measuring line across it? On what were its footings set, or who laid its cornerstone – while the morning stars sang together and all the angels shouted for joy?" (Job 38:3-7). God points out that we cannot understand him and he wouldn't be God if we did. His ways are not our ways.

When it comes to prayer for healing and wholeness, we must remember that there is no formula. You cannot be sure that if you do this and this, then that and that will happen. We have seen something of the wider world that we are living in, the spiritual forces and the effect of the fall that hamper the coming of the kingdom of God. Although this book is designed to ensure good practice and perhaps create the optimal conditions for healing and wholeness, God sometimes breaks all the "rules".

One area that our perspective sometimes diverges from God's is around the issue of death. As a teenager, I prayed for a close friend with metastatic (widespread) cancer. One night, after I had been praying for God to heal her, I had a picture. I was studying GCSE art at the time and had my watercolour paints out on my desk, so I stretched some paper and painted what I saw. It was of a large animal carcass, on its back, which had created a valley with the bones of the rib cage rising high as cliffs on either side. I saw a figure walking through the valley, along the spine of the carcass.

Beyond the valley, there was a beautiful land. I was so excited – surely, this was the valley of the shadow of death (Psalm 23) and the beautiful land ahead meant that God was going to heal my friend. Two days later, she died.

It has made me realise that sometimes, in some circumstances, death is a form of healing. It is notable that the Bible always refers to Christians "falling asleep" rather than dying. Just before Jesus raises Lazarus from death (John 11), he says to Lazarus' sister, Martha, "I am the resurrection and the life. The one who believes in me will live, even though they die; and whoever lives by believing in me will never die. Do you believe this?" (v.25-26). There is something here about living through dying that we don't really understand. In some situations, death is the way by which people are made more whole.

When Jesus was on the cross, he said to one of the men hanging with him, "Truly I tell you, today you will be with me in paradise" (Luke 23:43). In Acts 7:55-56, just as Stephen dies from stoning, we are told, "But Stephen, full of the Holy Spirit, looked up to heaven and saw the glory of God, and Jesus standing at the right hand of God. 'Look,' he said, 'I see heaven open and the Son of Man standing at the right hand of God.'" This is a picture of heaven and, as we have already seen, a place of power, healing and wholeness.

Finally, the Bible makes it clear that suffering will happen. We have already seen that it is a part of the world in which we live. Jesus said, "In this world you will have trouble. But take heart! I have overcome the world" (John 16:33). 1 Peter 5:10 says, "And the God of all grace, who called you to his eternal glory in Christ, after you have suffered a little while, will himself restore you and make you strong, firm and steadfast." Suffering for a little while is something that is inevitable for us all to some extent and may extend up to and including our death. It is also notable that Paul, who himself healed others, was not himself healed of his "thorn in the flesh" (2 Corinthians 12:7).

> **Exercise:**
>
> Reflect on and thank God that he is with us up to, including and beyond death.

Day 7: Reflection

It's time to rest, relax and reflect.

> "I lift up my eyes to the mountains –
> where does my help come from?
> My help comes from the Lord,
> the Maker of heaven and earth.
> He will not let your foot slip –
> he who watches over you will not slumber;
> indeed, he who watches over Israel
> will neither slumber nor sleep.
> The Lord watches over you –
> the Lord is your shade at your right hand;
> the sun will not harm you by day,
> nor the moon by night.
> The Lord will keep you from all harm –
> he will watch over your life;
> the Lord will watch over your coming and going
> both now and for evermore."
>
> (Psalm 121)

Thank God for his presence with you and his care for you.

Week 2: Group discussion questions

The list of questions below are suggestions only. The group may have other areas they wish to explore. Encourage group members to discuss and reflect on their experiences.

1. How have you found this week? Was there anything that surprised or struck you? Was there anything new or different? Is there anything that you didn't understand or disagreed with?
2. Read Luke 8:1-3 and verses 38-39. What was the response of those who had received healing? In what ways did it result in giving glory to God and devotion to service? Can you think of any similar examples from your own life where healing or wholeness has resulted in this?
3. Read Isaiah 58:6-12. What does this passage suggest are sometimes the pre-requisites for healing and wholeness? How should this impact on the work and service of our churches and organisations if we want them to be places of healing?
4. Why do you think Jesus asked people what they wanted him to do for them?

5. Praying with people can work synergistically with modern medicine. If you have a friend seeking medical advice or treatment for an illness, what things could you be praying for, other than healing from the illness itself?
6. Ephesians 1:13 refers to God marking those who believe in him with a seal, his promised Holy Spirit, that guarantees our inheritance. How does this make you feel?
7. The thought of spiritual battles and spiritual forces can be a little scary. How does Romans 8:38-39 reassure us? How can we support and reassure each other within the group?
8. Can you think of any examples in your own experience where death appears to have been a form of healing for someone? What do you think Jesus meant when he told the man on the cross next to him that "Truly I tell you, today you will be with me in paradise"?

As a group, read through the Lord's Prayer (e.g. Matthew 6:9-13) together slowly. Thinking about what we have studied this week, and the different types of healing (Appendix C), how does each line make this a prayer for wholeness and healing?

Week 3:

How do I pray for people who are sick?

Over the last two weeks we have explored whether we have a God who really cares and, if he cares, why we don't always see physical healing. We have looked at the role of spiritual forces and battles, the effect of the fall and the curse that the creation is under, the need to pray for the kingdom of God to come and his will to be done as part of praying for healing and wholeness. We have seen that even Jesus couldn't always do the miraculous things he wanted to. We have realised that God has a different perspective from ours.

We have done some spiritual warm-up exercises on finding our way to the foot of the cross and into the throne room of God.

We have worked through our own need for healing and wholeness. We have brought to God our own pain and problems from the past, sought forgiveness of our sins and help with forgiveness of others. We have encountered a God who loves deeply and is deeply moved in situations of distress.

We are now in a better position to start praying for others. We will spend the next two weeks looking at how we do this.

Day 1: Be whole

"May God himself, the God of peace, sanctify you through and through. May your whole spirit, soul and body be kept blameless at the coming of our Lord Jesus Christ. The one who calls you is faithful, and he will do it."
1 Thessalonians 5:23-24

How do we prepare ourselves for praying for others? There are probably two sorts of preparation. We need to be prepared on a daily basis for the unexpected need for someone who needs prayer for which we may have little or no time to prepare. Secondly, we may be asked to pray for someone at an agreed time in the future. In this instance, we have time to prepare.

In both instances, I would suggest that we need to spend time getting ourselves to the foot of the cross of Jesus. You already know how to do this and hopefully have been practising over the last two weeks. Once there, I would suggest we spend time asking the Holy Spirit to come and search us to show us the things for which we need to ask forgiveness, the people we need to forgive (or ask for God's help to forgive). We need to spend time praying for our own healing and wholeness first. We need to be made as whole as possible ourselves before we start praying for others. We also need to be filled with his Spirit.

> "I feel it to be of the utmost importance, that if he is to be used by our Lord as a channel of healing – a minister of healing Grace – he must himself be in a condition of wholeness. He certainly cannot be in that condition, unless he has made a sincere and careful preparation."
>
> Edgar Bell

If there is someone that you have been asked to pray with or pray for, we need to spend time thanking God that he knows the situation we will encounter so well already. He already cares, he already loves, he has compassion, power and love to meet their needs.

It is worth remembering that Jesus spent a considerable time in prayer alone himself. If he thought it important and valuable, how much more do we need to do it too? In Matthew 14 he spends the whole night alone praying before walking on water to join his disciples in the boat. In Mark 1, at the start of his ministry, we are told, "Very early in the morning, while it was still dark, Jesus got up, left the house and went off to a solitary place, where he prayed" (v.35).

In John 11:41-42, before raising Lazarus from the dead, Jesus says, "Father, I thank you that you have heard me. I knew that you always hear me, but I said this for

Day 1: Be whole

the benefit of the people standing here, that they may believe that you sent me." The miracle that follows results from a close relationship between Jesus and his Father in heaven. The same needs to be true for us too.

"Even when [preparation for praying for the healing of others] comes to be normal, [our] attitude must never be casual. An observer, who has been with me in all my work says this: 'I have noticed that whenever you have prepared yourself carefully for this work great things have followed your ministrations, but when for one reason or another you have not prepared with the same care, not so great things have happened.' It is as simple as that!"

Edgar Bell

Exercise:

Do you set aside time each day to spend with your Father in heaven? It doesn't need to be the same time each day if your routine varies. Think about when these times are and, it if helps, mark them as meetings in your diary.

Day 2: Be supported

"After this the Lord appointed seventy-two others and sent them two by two ahead of him to every town and place where he was about to go."
Luke 10:1

It's very interesting that Jesus never sent his disciples out alone. Nor did he send out the seventy-two ordinary folk like us on our own. In fact, Jesus himself never did anything on his own except perhaps the temptations in the desert and sometimes nights in prayer. We are not to do things on our own either. We are to pray for others in pairs. There are lots of very good reasons for this. We need to consider the safety of the person we are praying with and we need to keep ourselves safe too. We also often have gifts that complement the gifts of others – we may not have all the gifting that is needed for a particular case. So, always have a prayer buddy and the usual recommendation is that there should be one man and one woman praying for an individual.

We are reminded of this in Matthew 18:19-20 when Jesus says, "Again, truly I tell you that if two of you on earth agree about anything they ask for, it will be done for them by my Father in heaven. For where two or three gather in my name, there am I with them." So, if in doubt, take a third person too!

The story of the walk to Emmaus is an example of this. In Luke 24, two friends are walking along the road following the death and resurrection of Jesus and discussing everything that has happened. They are joined by a third – Jesus – who initially they do not recognise until supper. This is what happens when we pray for others in pairs. When two of us walk the journey together of prayer for healing and wholeness for others, we are often joined by Jesus who will walk with us.

> "He sent them out Two and Two, not singly, for He knew that this work of God could best be carried out in Fellowship."
>
> Edgar Bell

In James 5:13-16 we read, "Is anyone among you in trouble? Let them pray. Is anyone happy? Let them sing songs of praise. Is anyone among you ill? Let them call the elders of the church to pray over them and anoint them with oil in the name of the Lord. And the prayer offered in faith will make the sick person well; the Lord will raise them up. If they have sinned, they will be forgiven. Therefore confess your sins to each other and pray for each other so that you may be healed. The

Day 2: Be supported

prayer of a righteous person is powerful and effective." Again, the prayer here is by more than one person.

Finally, let's look at the biblical precedence for the process of "laying on of hands" during prayer for healing and wholeness. Before we do this, we need to remember that some people will not want to be touched and this must be respected.

In the Old Testament, Moses lays his hands on Joshua in commissioning him to take over the leadership of Israel (Numbers 27:18-23). This resulted in him being filled with wisdom and equipped for the job ahead (Deuteronomy 34:9). Laying a hand on the head of an animal was also an important part of the ritual for cleansing for unintentional sin (Leviticus 4). So there is a precedent here with the laying on of hands for empowering others for service for God and for cleansing from sin. Cleansing from sin, as we have seen, is an essential component of praying for healing and wholeness. Service for God is the usual purpose and result of healing.

In the New Testament, Jesus says, "And these signs will accompany those who believe: in my name they will drive out demons; they will speak in new tongues; they will pick up snakes with their hands; and when they drink deadly poison, it will not hurt them at all; they will place their hands on people who are ill, and they will get well" (Mark 16:17-18). So placing hands on sick people is a part of them getting well. However, Jesus himself did not always place hands on the people he healed.

Sometimes, they were healed some distance from where Jesus was.

In the Acts of the Apostles, laying on of hands on new believers was performed for them to receive the Holy Spirit (Acts 8:17), which again can be a part of the healing and wholeness process. Timothy was given his spiritual gifting when hands were laid on him (1 Timothy 4:14). In Acts 6:6 the seven appointed to take over the responsibility of caring for the Greek widows were commissioned for this service by being prayed for and having hands laid on them.

> ## Exercise:
> Has anyone ever laid hands on you and asked for God to fill you with his Spirit? If not, it is about time they did.

Day 3: Be careful

> "When he arrived at the house of Jairus, he did not let anyone go in with him except Peter, John and James, and the child's father and mother."
> Luke 8:51

We need to be careful with the context when we come to praying for people. Firstly, who else should be present other than the two prayer buddies? In the Bible verse today, we look at the raising from the dead of Jairus' daughter. Although Jesus did many healings in the middle of crowds, there were times when he was very careful about who was present. We notice in this Bible verse (and the similar accounts in Matthew and Mark), that he got rid of the crowds and the noise and took with him those "in the zone" – his three closest disciples and the child's parents. He removed everyone else.

In Mark 7:32-33 we are told, "There some people brought to him a man who was deaf and could hardly talk, and they begged Jesus to place his hand on him. After he took him aside, away from the crowd, Jesus put his fingers into the man's ears." Again, Jesus took the man aside, away from the crowd first and then healed him.

Reading through some of the miraculous healings collated by my great-grandfather, I was struck by two stories of children healed miraculously once the anxiety and the fear of the parents was dealt with first. In 1 Kings 17 Elijah raises the child of a widow after he has taken him upstairs and away from his mother. In 2 Kings 4 Elisha raises the Shunammite's son after, again, shutting the door on another anxious and angry mother. Jesus also sometimes dealt with issues from family members before proceeding to the healing miracle.

> "So often the hindrance to healing is to be found in the anxiety, fear, fussiness and worry of those who in affection are nearest to the patient."
>
> Edgar Bell

All of this tells us that there is something important about the context in which we pray for people. Like much in the healing and wholeness ministry, this will vary from situation to situation. We have already seen that we need to give up our claim on people when we pray for them. I think that some of these stories in the Bible are removing those who aren't "in the zone" and also removing those where their emotional claim is too strong. We hold onto those we love very tightly. It seems that sometimes, God needs to prise people out of our hands in order to get them into his, a bit like trying to prise out a favourite toy from the grip of a small child.

Day 3: Be careful

However, there are also plenty of examples of public healings in the Bible. There is clearly a purpose and a context for both. I would, however, suggest being careful when getting whole churches to pray for a sick individual. Although there is no doubt a time and a place for this, and we know that prayer is powerful and presumably enhanced with the number praying, if the individual is not healed in a way that some church members expect, they may be left with doubts as to whether God cares and, if he cares, whether he heals. We may end up unintentionally undermining their faith in a God who heals. They will not all understand the issues around wholeness rather than healing, spiritual battles, the need to pray for the kingdom of God and the will of God to be done.

Secondly, as we have seen, the person being prayed for usually must want to be healed. It is interesting that Jesus often asks people what they want him to do for them. He often made them articulate it. For example, in Luke 18:41 he says to a blind beggar, "'What do you want me to do for you?' 'Lord, I want to see,' he replied." However, sometimes it was an advocate for the person or, in the case of Jairus, the parent of the sick person, who is asking.

Thirdly, faith often leads to healing in ways we don't fully understand. For example, when the woman who has been bleeding for years touches Jesus' clothing, he tells her, "Daughter, your faith has healed you" (Mark 5:34). Similarly, the lepers who are healed in Luke 17 are told, "Your faith has made you well" (v.19). Jesus forgives the sins of the paralysed man and then physically heals him (Mark 2) because he "saw their faith". In the story of the healing of the centurion's servant in Luke 7, we are told, "When Jesus heard this, he was amazed at him, and turning to the crowd following him, he said, 'I tell you, I have not found such great faith even in Israel.' Then the men who had been sent returned to the house and found the servant well" (v.9-10).

It is notable that it is not necessarily the faith of the person who is sick that is needed. There are examples of people who are healed by Jesus because of the faith of others. Sometimes the faith is a little wobbly, like that of the parents of the child in Mark 9 who say to Jesus, "'But if you can do anything, take pity on us and help us.' '"If you can"?' said Jesus. 'Everything is possible for one who believes.' Immediately the boy's father exclaimed, 'I do believe; help me overcome my unbelief!'" (v.22-24). The child is healed. As we have seen, faith the size of a mustard seed is sufficient. In Matthew 21:22 Jesus says, "If you believe, you will receive whatever you ask for in prayer."

What is the faith that is needed? We are told in John 11:25-26 when Jesus talks to Martha about it, just before he raises Lazarus from the dead. "Jesus said to her, 'I am the resurrection and the life. The one who believes in me will live, even though they die; and whoever lives by believing in me will never die. Do you believe this?'"

We are not talking about a faith that God will do what we want him to in a given situation. It is a faith in Jesus who loved us, who died for us, who forgives us, who cares for us. It is entrusting ourselves or those we care for to him and relinquishing them completely into his care.

> "Let us be clear as to what exactly we mean by 'faith' . . . It can only be faith in the person of our Lord Jesus Christ, whose help is sought: faith in his redemptive love; faith that it is equal to all my need, or the need of my loved one."
>
> Edgar Bell

Exercise:

We all go through times when our faith is a little shaky. Think through those times and bring them to God in prayer. Ask for him to increase your faith.

Day 4: Be quiet

"The LORD said, 'Go out and stand on the mountain in the presence of the LORD, for the LORD is about to pass by.' Then a great and powerful wind tore the mountains apart and shattered the rocks before the LORD, but the LORD was not in the wind. After the wind there was an earthquake, but the LORD was not in the earthquake. After the earthquake came a fire, but the LORD was not in the fire. And after the fire came a gentle whisper. When Elijah heard it, he pulled his cloak over his face and went out and stood at the mouth of the cave."

1 Kings 19:11-13

So, here you are, with the person who wants prayer. You have prepared as well as possible and made yourself as whole as possible. You are with a prayer buddy who has done the same. What now? Firstly, make yourselves comfortable. I would suggest sitting with the person being prayed for in the middle and one buddy on each side, although often this is done standing. Then explain what you are going to do.

Explain that you are going to ask for the Holy Spirit to come. You may want to pray a short prayer for whatever it is they have asked for.

Ask for permission to place a hand on a shoulder. If they have come for healing for a problem in a particular part of their body, and if it is appropriate to do so, you may wish to place a hand on or near the area that needs physical healing.

Pray for the Holy Spirit to come. A simple, "Come, Holy Spirit," is sufficient.

Say a short opening prayer. Be specific. Don't ramble. One sentence is fine. This isn't about your words, it is about the person you care for encountering the God who loves them. The rule is to say as little as possible and get out of the way of God. Leave out "if you will". Pray again, "Come, Holy Spirit."

In the silence that follows, take that person to the foot of the cross of Jesus or into the throne room of God. Alternatively, Francis MacNutt suggests you ask Jesus to come into the room and take over. The important thing is that you take them to God and then you wait for him to minister to them.

Remember that God uses us in different ways in different situations. Sometimes God fills us with his Spirit and we impart his power to those who we are praying for. For example, sometimes our hand will become hot and the other person will feel its warmth. At other times, it is more like taking your friend to a medical appointment. You are there to make sure they get to the right place safely. You are there to come into the appointment with them. You are there to listen to what is being said and help interpret. You are there to help them kneel or sit (if you are standing) if they become unsteady.

Keep your ears open and your mouth shut. Wait, listen, watch, thank. If you (or your praying buddy) is given a picture or a word of knowledge, quietly, gently and kindly pass this on.

If you feel nothing is happening, ask the person you are praying for what they are thinking about. Remember, God may be dealing directly with them and not at all via you.

At the end, leave them in the presence of God – encourage them to continue letting God do whatever he is doing. They don't have to leave the room when you have finished praying with them – they can stay. Quite frankly, once they are established, safe and comfortable in the presence of God and the Holy Spirit is at work, you are sometimes no longer needed. You can move to the next person.

> "Keep in mind that the Cross is the symbol and proof of God's love, and therefore, the one safe place for all children of God. I would find a place of quiet, kneel down; close my eyes and cover my ears that no other sight or sound may intrude. I would wait until I am quite composed and still. Then I would ask for the guidance of the Holy Spirit, and

At the Foot of the Cross

try to picture again the Great Event which took place on Calvary. I do not forget that many cannot think in pictures. Let them use their own method as long as it achieves the purpose, that is, brings them to the Cross. I concentrate on the Person of the suffering Saviour until He and He alone is There. When this has been achieved, I then bring both the patient and myself into the picture. The patient because of his great need of redemptive healing and wholeness; myself, because I, too, stand in need of that redemptive love, without which I cannot hope to be of service to the sufferer."

Edgar Bell

"So, then, we are both brought within the scope of the great Redemptive act, and since there is no more that I can do, I leave my patient there, at the foot of the Cross, asking nothing, but just placing him at God's disposal, who alone knows his need and who alone can adequately meet it."

Edgar Bell

Exercise:

In the text above, Edgar describes his method for praying for someone to be healed expecting that we should do likewise. We've tried this before but try it again – these things take practice!

Day 5: Be humble

"As he went along, he saw a man blind from birth. His disciples asked him, 'Rabbi, who sinned, this man or his parents, that he was born blind?' 'Neither this man nor his parents sinned,' said Jesus, 'but this happened so that the works of God might be displayed in him.'"
John 9:1-3

There are times when we pray for others that we get things completely wrong. In this case, the disciples assumed that the illness was being caused by sin. It was not. Getting things wrong from time to time is inevitable. We are being brave and entering into a world of things that we cannot see and do not understand. We are only human! It's ok to get things wrong. But be humble. Be kind, be brave and be prepared to apologise.

Firstly, *avoid assumptions*. For example, there will be people who you want to pray for but who do not themselves want prayer. There are all sorts of reasons for this. Sometimes it is very simply that they feel they are already exactly where God wants them to be because of or despite their sickness or suffering. It is interesting that Jesus always asked people whether they wanted to be healed. He never assumed it and nor should we. Accept the "no". If someone doesn't want you to put a hand on them or doesn't want prayer, they don't need to justify it. You need to get on with the job in hand and ensure you are working within their comfort zone as much as possible (accepting, of course, that encountering Jesus is frequently not within our comfort zones).

Secondly, *listen, listen and listen again.* Listen carefully to the person asking for prayer. They need to talk out the problem. Don't feel the need to jump into prayer straight away. Sometimes talking out a problem is part of the healing. However, the alternative also happens. Sometimes people don't want to tell you the reason they've asked for prayer. You don't need to know why someone is asking for prayer. God knows it all and that is sufficient. You are there to help them encounter God and he will do the rest. One of the things that Job's friends got right was when they "sat on the ground with him for seven days and seven nights. No one said a word to him, because they saw how great his suffering was" (Job 2:13). Sometimes we need to sit on the ground with people before trying to solve the problem.

Then listen, listen and listen again to God. You need to get used to hearing and recognising his voice. This takes time, patience, practice and usually some mentoring.

Day 5: Be humble

Francis MacNutt, in his book *The Practice of Healing Prayer*, recommends that we pray around the issues. For example, if you are praying for someone with cancer, pray that the cancer will regress and go away. But also pray that the effects of the treatment will be enhanced through prayer and pray against the side effects. In my experience, disseminated cancer rarely goes away completely when prayed for, although very occasionally, this does happen. What is much more common when we pray is that pain reduces, side effects subside and life is extended.

Thirdly, *don't be afraid to ask for help*. I remember praying for a woman once at a Christian conference who had come forward during a time of ministry with pain. That wasn't unusual – many people come forward with all sorts of pain. After praying with her for a while, I asked her how the pain was. Much worse, she told me. At that point I felt I was out of my depth. At the time, because of the volume of people coming forward for prayer, we were praying on a one-to-one basis but with two people appointed for directing and supporting what was happening rather than doing the praying. We had a signal that if we needed help we would put a hand in the air. My hand went straight up in the air. I waited for help. My sister Juliet happened to be on the same prayer team that year and was the first to answer. She started praying for the woman too. After a little longer, her pain began to subside.

The important thing here is that we need to be willing to be used for healing but accept that God may not use us. Remember, we need to be obedient and leave the results to him. We also need to be prepared to ask for help.

Fourthly, *say what you see but be prepared that you may have got it wrong*. There are times when I have a clear picture whilst praying for someone which means nothing at all to the person I am praying for. Give pictures and words of knowledge with care and humility. You may never find out if they meant something to the person you gave them to. Again, you don't need to know. This is about that person and God, not you.

It's also worth remembering that we bring our own assumptions, experiences and prejudices into a situation. We need to be aware of that and remember it's not what we think that counts, it is what God thinks.

Fifthly, *be very wary of creating power dynamics*. The person coming forward for prayer is not coming to you because of your authority and expertise. They are coming to God because of his. Stand to the side of them, not in front. Watch your body language when you are praying. Avoid authoritative "power" gestures such as pushing back on their forehead. Remember, this is not your ministry. This is God's. It is into his power and for his glory we do this, not our own. We are going through this as companion and friend to the person coming for prayer – we are in this together with them.

As 1 Peter 5:5-7 says, "All of you, clothe yourselves with humility towards one another, because, 'God opposes the proud but shows favour to the humble.' Humble yourselves, therefore, under God's mighty hand, that he may lift you up in due time. Cast all your anxiety on him because he cares for you."

> ### Exercise:
> Ask God to open your eyes and ears to his voice and direction and then spend some time in quiet, learning to listen to him. Again – this takes practice so be patient.

Day 6: Be cleansed

> "For our struggle is not against flesh and blood, but against the rulers, against the authorities, against the powers of this dark world and against the spiritual forces of evil in the heavenly realms."
>
> Ephesians 6:12

When you have finished praying for the person or people you have been ministering to, find some space for yourself for debriefing and washing off. Ideally, find someone else who has not been involved in the person or people you've been praying for who can pray for you and debrief you. Ensure that the debriefing does not break confidentiality unless an issue has arisen that requires reporting (see Week 6). Aim to explore the feeling and experiences of the one praying.

There are two aspects to this. Firstly, we need spiritually washing off. As the Ephesians 6 passage points out, our struggles are not against things we can see, but things we cannot. You will have seen by reading this far that some illness and brokenness is emotional and spiritual. We do not know which spiritual battles we are engaging in when we pray for people. We may think we are only praying for a sore knee or a stomach ache, but there may be a whole spiritual world we have been involved in during our prayer time that we are (blissfully!) unaware of. You don't need to be frightened of this, but you do need to be wise. You need a spiritual shower after crawling through the spiritual mud. You need to make sure that none of the mud sticks and doesn't affect you in the future.

The way I suggest you do this is to ask someone independent from the battles you've been involved in to pray for you to be spiritually washed off. Some involved in Christian healing recommend praying for a spiritual Teflon coating, so that nothing sticks.

The verse from Ephesians 6 today comes from the passage on putting on the armour of God. We are engaged in spiritual battles and we need to be equipped in spiritual clothing. We are told, "Finally, be strong in the Lord and in his mighty power. Put on the full armour of God, so that you can take your stand against the devil's schemes" (v.10-11). The passage describes the armour of God: "Stand firm then, with the belt of truth buckled around your waist, with the breastplate of righteousness in place, and with your feet fitted with the readiness that comes from the gospel of peace. In addition to all this, take up the shield of faith, with which you can extinguish all the flaming arrows of the evil one. Take the helmet of salvation and the sword of the Spirit, which is the word of God. And pray in the Spirit on all occasions with all kinds of prayers and requests" (v.14-18).

Secondly, at the end of praying, debrief. We can learn a lot from each other as we discuss the experiences we've had whilst praying for people. We can discuss things that have worked and haven't worked or difficulties that we have encountered. We can discuss words of knowledge that we've had and the things we aren't sure of. This period of debriefing can function as really good learning for all. Remember, though, to maintain confidentiality.

It's worth noting that Jesus himself debriefed the seventy-two ordinary folk after sending them out. Luke 10:17-20 states, "The seventy-two returned with joy and said, 'Lord, even the demons submit to us in your name.' He replied, 'I saw Satan fall like lightning from heaven. I have given you authority to trample on snakes and scorpions and to overcome all the power of the enemy; nothing will harm you. However, do not rejoice that the spirits submit to you, but rejoice that your names are written in heaven.'"

When we are obedient to God, he gives us what we need, and the authority required, to do the job he is asking us to do. He has commanded us to pray for others to be healed. We need to get on and do it.

But it isn't always easy, especially when nothing appears to happen. We trust that something always happens when we pray but we don't always know what's happened. We need to take the risk, and trust God for the rest. We need to remember to hand over our friend into God's hands in faith that God knows, cares and understands "God times" more than we do.

Sometimes we need to say, like the parent of the child who couldn't be healed by the disciples, "I do believe; help me overcome my unbelief!" (Mark 9:24).

Finally, as part of the debriefing, we may wish to consider the reasons why people are not healed elucidated by Francis MacNutt in his book *Healing*. We will go into these in more detail in Week 5.

Exercise:

Read through, reflect and pray through Ephesians 6:10-20.

Day 7: Reflection

It's time to rest, relax and reflect.

"Whoever dwells in the shelter of the Most High
will rest in the shadow of the Almighty.
I will say of the LORD, 'He is my refuge and my fortress,
my God, in whom I trust.'
Surely he will save you
from the fowler's snare
and from the deadly pestilence.
He will cover you with his feathers,
and under his wings you will find refuge."

(Psalm 91:1-4)

Thank God that he provides refuge for us when things are tough.

Week 3: Group discussion questions

The list of questions below are suggestions only. The group may have other areas they wish to explore. Encourage group members to discuss and reflect on their experiences.

1. How have you found this week? Was there anything that surprised or struck you? Was there anything new or different? Is there anything that you didn't understand or disagreed with?
2. Jesus spent a lot of time in prayer. What are our prayer lives like? Do we prepare for things by spending time in prayer? If so, when do we do this? Are there other times when we should do this but we don't? What stops us?
3. What are your thoughts and experience of praying in twos for someone else rather than on our own? Why do you think Jesus sent people out in twos?
4. Read John 11:25-27. The issue of faith has sometimes been misunderstood when it comes to healing and wholeness. What is it that we are asked to have faith in and how does this affect how we pray? (Note: The John passage

points us to the death and resurrection of Jesus – it brings us back to the foot of the cross and faith in the power of Jesus to make all things whole. You may find it easier to read it in the wider context of the story of the raising of Lazarus.)

5. In Luke 10:20, when the seventy-two that Jesus has sent out return to him, Jesus says, "However, do not rejoice that the spirits submit to you, but rejoice that your names are written in heaven." Why do you think he says this?

6. Why is humility so important when praying for healing and wholeness in others? What assumptions and prejudices may we unconsciously bring into a situation? How can we become more aware of them?

7. Why is debriefing important? How can we do this practically?

8. Read Ephesians 6:10-20. How can we use this passage to prepare for prayer?

If you can, as a group, separate into groups of three. Two people practise praying for the third person as described in Day 4. Be quiet. Each time, wait for the Holy Spirit to come. When you are ready, change to the next person. If you feel able to, discuss your experiences at the end.

Week 4:

What else do I need to think about?

Last week, we built on our spiritual and theological understanding of healing and wholeness in looking at practical aspects of how you actually go about the task of praying for someone for healing and wholeness. We have looked at personal preparation, having a prayer buddy, being careful, quiet and humble, and spiritual showering at the end.

But if this is going to be more than a one-off prayer for others, we need to think more widely about other activities we may need to engage in. We will look at these this week.

Day 1: Be rested

"He came to a broom bush, sat down under it and prayed that he might die. 'I have had enough, LORD,' he said. 'Take my life; I am no better than my ancestors.' Then he lay down under the bush and fell asleep."
1 Kings 19:4-5

Elijah had had an exhausting time. He had met up with the prophets of Baal on Mount Carmel and set up a "whose God is greater" test which had relied on God doing something instantaneous and amazing at exactly the right time. He had then put his face between his knees and prayed fervently for rain, sending his servant seven times to see whether he could see any rain clouds. He then sprinted ahead of Ahab (who presumably was on wheels) all the way to Jezreel. After all of that, he then had to run for his life. No wonder that, at this point in time, he came to a broom bush, sat down and prayed that he might die. He must have been completely spiritually, emotionally and physically exhausted.

We may not have to go through quite what Elijah did, but we will still find that ministry (including praying for others) can be completely exhausting. We need to expect this and plan for it. Arrange rest times after prayer times.

Even Jesus found that ministry can be costly. In Luke 8:42-46 we are told, "As Jesus was on his way, the crowds almost crushed him. And a woman was there who had been subject to bleeding for twelve years, but no one could heal her. She came up behind him and touched the edge of his cloak, and immediately her bleeding stopped. 'Who touched me?' Jesus asked. When they all denied it, Peter said, 'Master, the people are crowding and pressing against you.' But Jesus said, 'Someone touched me; I know that power has gone out from me.'" Jesus felt some of the energy from power leave. How exhausted he must have been when he had been healing and undertaking ministry for days on end!

Perhaps, unsurprisingly, Jesus needed sleep and rest away from the crowds. In Mark 4 he leaves the crowds behind, takes his disciples and gets into a boat. The boat goes through a storm but Jesus manages to sleep through it all. We are told, "A furious squall came up, and the waves broke over the boat, so that it was nearly swamped. Jesus was in the stern, sleeping on a cushion" (v.37-38). He must have been in a deep sleep from an exhausting day.

Perhaps it is not surprising that he often withdrew to lonely places after administering to crowds and healing them. Luke 5:15-16 states, "Yet the news about him spread all the more, so that crowds of people came to hear him and to be healed of their illnesses. But Jesus often withdrew to lonely places and prayed." We sometimes need to withdraw too, to rest, recuperate and then prepare for whatever comes next.

He also advised his disciples to get rest. In Mark 6:30-31 we are told, "The apostles gathered round Jesus and reported to him all they had done and taught. Then, because so many people were coming and going that they did not even have a chance to eat, he said to them, 'Come with me by yourselves to a quiet place and get some rest.'"

If, after periods of fervent and persistent praying, we feel like we need a rest, don't be surprised. If Elijah needed it, Jesus needed and the disciples needed it, you will need it too – and probably in a double dose.

Finally, don't be afraid to ask for prayer yourself. When it comes to prayer for healing and wholeness, as Christians, we are a group of friends helping each other out along the parts of the path of life which are difficult to walk along alone. Although some are more experienced and gifted helpers than others, we all encounter stony, rocky and thorny parts of the path of life. Don't be too proud to be the one to ask for prayer.

Remember, this is God's ministry we take part in. Not ours. We are part of his team working under him in his power and to his glory. In Matthew 11:28-30 Jesus says, "Come to me, all you who are weary and burdened, and I will give you rest. Take my yoke upon you and learn from me, for I am gentle and humble in heart, and you will find rest for your souls. For my yoke is easy and my burden is light."

Exercise:

Spend time just resting in God's presence today. Try to rest your mind and enjoy his refreshment, love and care. Try not to achieve anything but rest and relaxation.

Day 2: Be persistent

"Let us not become weary in doing good, for at the proper time we will reap a harvest if we do not give up."
Galatians 6:9

When we pray for someone to be healed, persistence is everything. Too often we go in to praying for someone wanting something big, dramatic and instantaneous to happen. We live in an impatient society where we want things ever quicker and with little effort. This is contrary to the way healing prayer generally works. Although God does occasionally work with big, sudden miracles, we need to realise that this is the exception rather than the rule. In most instances of healing prayer, people are healed gradually, over time, and with persistent prayer.

Healing is usually *a process rather than an event.* It occurs slowly over time rather than suddenly. We more often see very small steps and small improvements which accumulate gradually as we pray.

It is worth remembering the story of the angel coming in answer to Daniel's prayer (Daniel 10). Daniel had prayed persistently for three weeks. During these three weeks, the angel had been detained and was ultimately released. Would Daniel still have received an answer if he had prayed just once? I think not. We cannot see the spiritual battles that we engage in when we pray, so keep going.

Jesus also urged us to be persistent in prayer. For example, at the start of the parable of the persistent widow in Luke 18:1-8, we are told, "Then Jesus told his disciples a parable to show them that they should always pray and not give up." In the parable of the persistent neighbour in Luke 11, the neighbour eventually gets up to give his friend the bread that is needed because of the persistence and "shameless audacity" (v.8) of the one asking.

Elijah was someone else who was persistent in prayer. In James 5:17-18, we are told, "Elijah was a human being, even as we are. He prayed earnestly that it would not rain, and it did not rain on the land for three and a half years. Again, he prayed, and the heavens gave rain, and the earth produced its crops." Note the words "He prayed earnestly". We need to do the same.

In Mark 9 Jesus heals a demon-possessed boy who the disciples were unable to heal. The boy's parents came to Jesus very frustrated, and he was able to do what his disciples had not. The explanation that he gives them is, "This kind can come out only by prayer" (v.29). We don't really know what this means, except that it is again a call to faithful prayer.

I was praying for someone recently with a long-term physical problem. I have noticed something. The weeks and months when I have prayed, my friend gets a gradual improvement in symptoms. The weeks and months when I give up and get distracted or frustrated, things seem to slowly get worse again. Eventually, I start praying again because things are bad and things slowly start to improve again. Maybe, if I kept going in faithful prayer, it would disappear completely. I am about to find out.

It reminds me of story of the Israelite army fighting the Amalekites in Exodus 17:8-15. Joshua was leading the battle. Moses was standing on top of the hill overlooking it with the staff of God in his hands. We are told, "As long as Moses held up his hands, the Israelites were winning, but whenever he lowered his hands, the Amalekites were winning. When Moses' hands grew tired, they took a stone and put it under him, and he sat on it. Aaron and Hur held his hands up – one on one side, one on the other – so that his hands remained steady till sunset" (v.11-12). At sunset, the battle was done and the Amalekites were defeated. Presumably, Moses' arms and hands had a well-deserved break.

It is worth remembering that, traditionally, prayer involves the raising of hands. We see this in Psalm 63:4 and Psalm 141:2 as well as in 1 Timothy 2:8. Here in the West, we tend to think of people who raise their hands in prayer and worship as doing something new.

They are not. Raising hands in prayer is as they did in the Old Testament and continue to do in some Middle Eastern cultures.

It is also worth noting that Moses couldn't sustain this alone – he needed help and so might we. Keeping up sustained prayer can be tiring and exhausting. Again, this isn't something we should be doing alone.

In his books on healing, Francis MacNutt introduced the idea of the "soaking" prayer.[4] He noticed that praying for hours, sometimes days or weeks, as slowly, slowly, small changes happen that lead to improvement. When we soak people in prayer, we pray with them and for them for prolonged and sustained periods of time, seeing improvement little by little.

"Wait for the LORD; be strong and take heart and wait for the LORD" (Psalm 27:14).

Exercise:

Make Psalm 63:1-8 your prayer today. Read, reflect and pray through it.

---

4. MacNutt, *The Practice of Healing Prayer.*

Day 3: Be thankful

"Though the fig-tree does not bud and there are no grapes on the vines, though the olive crop fails and the fields produce no food, though there are no sheep in the sheepfold and no cattle in the stalls, yet I will rejoice in the LORD, I will be joyful in God my Saviour."
Habakkuk 3:17-18

Thankfulness to God is so important when it comes to healing and wholeness. But it can be a decision of will rather than a natural emotional reaction. There are times when we will see very little happen despite our ardent, most fervent and persistent prayers, and will need to, like Habakkuk, say, "Yet I will rejoice . . ."

We believe and trust that when we pray, something always happens. However, we do not always see the fruit of our prayers. Sometimes we have to choose to thank God for what we cannot see and do not know, but we trust and believe that God is at work. Unlike Daniel, we do not know which demons and angels may be involved in whatever is going on.

Habakkuk was not the only person in the Bible to praise and worship despite his circumstances – it's quite a common theme. We see it in the psalms and in Job. When Job had lost everything – his family, his possessions, his wealth – we are told, "At this, Job got up and tore his robe and shaved his head. Then he fell to the ground in worship and said: 'Naked I came from my mother's womb, and naked I will depart. The LORD gave and the LORD has taken away; may the name of the LORD be praised'" (Job 1:20-21). Shaving our head and tearing are clothes are optional in our day and age, but choosing to praise God is not.

1 Thessalonians 5:16-18 urges us to "Rejoice always, pray continually, give thanks in all circumstances". Not easy to do, especially when the going is tough and we are exhausted. Note that we should be thankful *in* all circumstances not *for* all circumstances. God is always worthy of our praise and worship, whatever our circumstances.

What should we be thanking God for? I would suggest the following for starters:

1. Thank God that he loves and cares for us. Thank him for his presence. Thank him for his power. Thank him for his compassion. Thank him for sending Jesus. Thank him for the cross.

2. Thank him for the small gains that you see when you pray for healing and wholeness. For example, Francis MacNutt[5] suggests there are

---

5. MacNutt, *The Practice of Healing Prayer*.

Day 3: Be thankful

three things to look out for when praying for physical healing:

a. Pain – will decrease even if the underlying cause (e.g. cancer) stays

b. Mobility – will increase

c. Structure – deformity corrects

You may see other things too – a sense of peace developing in someone you are praying for, an acceptance of a situation, a new way through, an improvement in difficult relationships, etc.

It is worth remembering the story in Luke 17 where Jesus heals ten lepers. He told them to go and show themselves to the priests. As they went, they were healed of their leprosy. We are then told, "One of them, when he saw he was healed, came back, praising God in a loud voice. He threw himself at Jesus' feet and thanked him – and he was a Samaritan. Jesus asked, 'Were not all ten cleansed? Where are the other nine? Has no one returned to give praise to God except this foreigner?'" (v.15-18). The story shows the importance of thankfulness.

Exercise:

Today, count your blessings. How many can you name in ten seconds? Then thank God for all those you've thought of.

Day 4: Be lovely

"If I speak in the tongues of men or of angels, but do not have love, I am only a resounding gong or a clanging cymbal. If I have the gift of prophecy and can fathom all mysteries and all knowledge, and if I have a faith that can move mountains, but do not have love, I am nothing. If I give all I possess to the poor and give over my body to hardship that I may boast but do not have love, I gain nothing."

1 Corinthians 13:1-3

It is quite common – in fact, I would argue normal – for the gifts of the Spirit, particularly speaking in tongues, gifts of prophecy and words of knowledge, to be used in prayer for healing and wholeness. This doesn't mean for a minute that you must have any of these gifts, but simply to expect their use. 1 Thessalonians 5:19-22 warns us to use them but be sensible about them: "Do not quench the Spirit. Do not treat prophecies with contempt but test them all; hold on to what is good, reject every kind of evil."

But the Bible is clear – whatever we do, we need to do it with love. We can have gifts beyond all measure, but if we don't use them in a way that is loving, then they are wasted. In fact, more than wasted – things are changed for the worse. We gain nothing. We are nothing.

The Greek word for love used in this context is *"agape"*. This differs from other words for love used in the Bible such as those that refer to brotherly or sisterly affection and erotic love. *Agape* is the same word that is used to describe God's love for us. It is used in John 15:9 when Jesus says, "As the Father has loved me, so have I loved you. Now remain in my love", and again in verses 12-13, which say, "My command is this: love each other as I have loved you. Greater love has no one than this: to lay down one's life for one's friends." *Agape* describes a love that is unconditional, sustaining and often divine.

We have looked at the physical context in which we might pray for someone, but this is the spiritual one. We pray for each other for healing and wholeness with an attitude and process which is encompassed entirely with *"agape"* love. Otherwise, we become annoying gongs and clanging symbols that cause problems rather than solve them.

How do we develop this sort of love? How do we become the sort of people who can create this spiritual context? Well, you won't be surprised to read that the first thing we must do is to become as whole as possible, by bringing ourselves regularly to the foot of the cross of Jesus. We need to be honest with the past and the present, the things we have done wrong or failed to do, and the people we need to forgive.

Then, as you would expect by now, we need to pray for the Holy Spirit to make us more like Jesus. *"Agape"* love is a fruit of the Holy Spirit recorded in Galatians 5:22-23, which says, "But the fruit of the Spirit is love, joy, peace, forbearance, kindness, goodness, faithfulness, gentleness and self-control." These fruits create the context for prayer for healing and wholeness.

We need to keep in a right relationship with God as much as possible. In John 15:4-5 Jesus commands us to "Remain in me, as I also remain in you. No branch can bear fruit by itself; it must remain in the vine. Neither can you bear fruit unless you remain in me. I am the vine; you are the branches. If you remain in me and I in you, you will bear much fruit; apart from me you can do nothing".

We become fruitful by being as close to Jesus as possible. By remaining in him, our prayers will be answered. "If you remain in me and my words remain in you, ask whatever you wish, and it will be done for you. This is to my Father's glory, that you bear much fruit, showing yourselves to be my disciples" (John 15:7-8). Note again that this results in bringing glory to God.

In praying for others, we are expressing our faith in a God who loves us, through our action of praying for the healing and wholeness of others. As Galatians 5:6 says, "The only thing that counts is faith expressing itself through love." In James 2 we are also urged to express our faith through practical action.

Practical action also involves reflecting on our times praying with others to work out what went well and what we could do differently next time, apologising when we get things wrong, and giving whatever thoughts or messages we think are appropriate with an immense amount of kindness and humility.

> **Exercise:**
>
> Spend time naming and then praying for an increase in each fruit of the Spirit.

Day 5: Be mentored

"Jesus went up on a mountainside and called to him those he wanted, and they came to him. He appointed twelve that they might be with him and that he might send them out to preach and to have authority to drive out demons."
Mark 3:13-15

Mentorship is really important in prayer ministry. Certainly, I have valued having someone more experienced than me who I can debrief with, ask questions and better understand situations from a spiritual perspective. I've learnt a lot through mentoring and it has helped and improved my practice and continues to do so.

Jesus was a mentor to his disciples. They spent three years with him watching what he did and how he did it, listening to him speak and asking questions. He then sent them out to try doing things more independently. After sending out the twelve, he sent out the seventy-two and, again, trained, mentored and debriefed. They discussed their experiences with him on their return (Luke 10:17).

When we are learning to pray for others for healing and wholeness, mentoring works at several different levels. Firstly, we are being mentored and guided by the Holy Spirit, learning from the Bible what we should do and how we should do it and allowing God to lead us and guide us. As Jesus said, "All this I have spoken while still with you. But the Advocate, the Holy Spirit, whom the Father will send in my name, will teach you all things and will remind you of everything I have said to you" (John 14:25-26).

Secondly, we benefit from mentoring from another Christian or Christians who have more experience than we do in prayer for healing and wholeness. As we gain more experience, we will find ourselves encountering things we haven't had to understand before. It can be difficult, for example, to work out whether someone who is screaming or shaking violently during an encounter with the Holy Spirit is having a manifestation of the Holy Spirit, suffering a psychiatric or neurological episode, or there is some sort of demonic involvement. This isn't the sort of thing you want to be handling alone – you want to be with someone who recognises the symptoms of the underlying problem and will teach how to recognise it and what to do about it. This comes only with experience. In a sense, it's learning the art of medicine in a different form.

Thirdly, we need to be mentors to others. The apostles, having been mentored by Jesus, mentored others as seen in the Acts of the Apostles, and we should do the same. Sometimes, we are learning together. As

Galatians says, "Carry each other's burdens, and in this way you will fulfil the law of Christ. If anyone thinks they are something when they are not, they deceive themselves. Each one should test their own actions. Then they can take pride in themselves alone, without comparing themselves to someone else, for each one should carry their own load. Nevertheless, the one who receives instruction in the word should share all good things with their instructor" (Galatians 6:2-6).

Exercise:

Reflect back on people who have mentored and taught you in your Christian life. What did they do or say that was helpful? Is there anyone who can support and mentor you as you start praying for others? Pray through all of this today.

Day 6: Be integrated

"Just as a body, though one, has many parts, but all its many parts form one body, so it is with Christ. For we were all baptised by one Spirit so as to form one body – whether Jews or Gentiles, slave or free – and we were all given the one Spirit to drink. And so the body is not made up of one part but of many."
1 Corinthians 12:12-14

Christian healing prayer usually (but not always) occurs within a wider Christian community. It is important that where possible it does so for two reasons.

Firstly, those coming forward for prayer often need wider support. They may need regular persistent ongoing prayer from a small group of Christians in order, like Moses, for the arms of prayer to be held up until the end of the battle. Many churches have groups, variously referred to as "home groups", "cell groups" or "small groups", which are groups of people who study the Bible, discuss and pray together. They can be a fabulous place of love and support for their members and are certainly one way that prayer for individuals may be maintained over a prolonged period.

We are urged to "Carry each other's burdens, and in this way you will fulfil the law of Christ" (Galatians 6:2). Carrying each other's burdens includes carrying people in prayer to the foot of the cross of Jesus, where they can be made whole and where broken things in their lives can be put back together again.

Integration with other church groups and activities may all form part of the healing process. For example, those seeking healing may benefit from going on an Alpha course (which goes through the basics of Christian faith with talks and discussion), a parenting course, joining a bereavement support group, a parent and toddler group or coffee and craft. We need to remember that wholeness is not just about physical healing; it is much wider, greater and deeper than that and is fundamentally relational at heart. When made whole, we are brought into right relationship with God and, often, with others.

There may, of course, be a need for professional help from outside of the church community. This may include medical help with physical problems, mental health support and treatment, counselling services and social care support.

Similarly, those needing prayer may benefit from the spiritual gifts from the wider community. As 1 Corinthians 12:4-6 says, "There are different kinds of gifts, but the same Spirit distributes them. There are different kinds of service, but the same Lord. There are different kinds of working, but in all of them and in everyone it is the same God at work." We are meant to work and serve within communities.

The body of Christ passage is relevant here. As part of the community of God, what affects and hurts one of us, affects us all. "But God has put the body together, giving greater honour to the parts that lacked it, so that there should be no division in the body, but that its parts should have equal concern for each other. If one part suffers, every part suffers with it; if one part is honoured, every part rejoices with it" (1 Corinthians 12:24-26).

Secondly, integration into a wider Christian community is helpful as the purposes of healing, as we have seen, is to bring glory to God and to bring the person into the service of Christ. If someone is to serve Christ, it is likely they will do so as part of the work of the Christian community in which they are a part.

Exercise:

If you are part of a small group of Christians, as part of a prayer group, home group or cell group for example, think about what skills and gifts each other member is contributing. How does or could the mix of the gifts and skills be used for service to others?

Day 7: Reflection

It's time to rest, relax and reflect.

"The LORD is my shepherd, I lack nothing.
He makes me lie down in green pastures,
he leads me beside quiet waters,
he refreshes my soul.
He guides me along the right paths
for his name's sake.
Even though I walk
through the darkest valley,
I will fear no evil,
for you are with me;
your rod and your staff,
they comfort me.
You prepare a table before me
in the presence of my enemies.
You anoint my head with oil;
my cup overflows.
Surely your goodness and love will follow me
all the days of my life,
and I will dwell in the house of the LORD
for ever."

(Psalm 23)

Thank God for his refreshment and comfort.

Week 4: Group discussion questions

The list of questions below are suggestions only. The group may have other areas they wish to explore. Encourage group members to discuss and reflect on their experiences.

1. How have you found this week? Was there anything that surprised or struck you? Was there anything new or different? Is there anything that you didn't understand or disagreed with?
2. Read 1 Kings 19:3-9. What happened to Elijah? How did God minister to him? Have you ever got to the point of being completely exhausted? How did you react? What helped you to recover? Do you think that God ministers to you too?
3. Do you find it easier to pray for others or ask for prayer for yourself? Why do you think that is?
4. Healing is usually a process rather than an event. How does this affect how we should pray? How can we sustain prayer over a long period of time? What are the challenges? How can we "soak" people in prayer?

5. We are told to "Rejoice always, pray continually, give thanks in all circumstances" (1 Thessalonians 5:16-18). When things are difficult, how easy is it to continue to thank God? What can we continue to thank him for?

6. Read Habakkuk 1:2-4 then 3:16-18. Do we ever feel like Habakkuk did? What can we learn from these verses for when we face difficult times?

7. Think about your own experience of mentoring and training, either as the trainee or the trainer. What are the similarities and differences to how Jesus trained and mentored his disciples?

As a group, read through Appendix D: Glossary of Spiritual Gifts. Can each member of the group identify their own gifting? Can you help each other identify theirs? How do your giftings contribute to the body of Christ and to your church/organisation?

Are there members of the group or known to the group who need healing/wholeness at the moment? Can the group find ways of "soaking" the individual or individuals over a prolonged period of time in prayer? Watch for the small gains over the next few weeks from this process.

Part 2

Organisational Context

Week 5:

What is the role of the sacraments and other church traditions in healing and wholeness?

Depending on your church background, you may feel quite strongly in favour or against the idea of sacraments and other church traditions in the Christian healing ministry. I include a week on it here because there is no doubt that many people have been suddenly and miraculously healed at the point of receiving a sacrament, even if it is not expressed in this way within their own church culture.

Jesus himself used practical actions and imagery to reveal and demonstrate spiritual truths and this included the times when he healed people.

There is a lot of debate around aspects of the sacraments between church tradition. I intend to avoid all areas of contention during this week's reflections. As usual, the only question we need to answer for our purposes is this one: what do we need to understand about the sacraments to pray for healing for others?

If you wish to read more about the history and theology of the sacraments, please see the "Further reading" section at the end.

Day 1: Sacraments in healing – why bother?

"Naaman's servants went to him and said, 'My father, if the prophet had told you to do some great thing, would you not have done it? How much more, then, when he tells you, "Wash and be cleansed"!' So he went down and dipped himself in the Jordan seven times, as the man of God had told him, and his flesh was restored and became clean like that of a young boy."

2 Kings 5:13-14

A sacrament is a visible symbol or sign of an invisible spiritual process or event. They are, as we see in healing, a means of God's power and love as well as a symbol of it. Andrew Davison, in his book *Why Sacraments?*,[6] describes sacraments as occasions when Christ reaches out to us. He continues to explain how Jesus' life was sacramental – he constantly used actions, practical signs, imagery and pictures to reveal spiritual truths.

---

6. Andrew Davison, *Why Sacraments?* (London: SPCK, 2013).

For example, in Jesus' healing ministry he tells the paralysed man to get up and pick up his mat (Luke 5:24), tells ten men with leprosy to go and show themselves to the priest (Luke 17:14), he uses spit and mud for a blind man and then tells him to go and wash in the Pool of Siloam (John 9:6-7) and he tells a man with a shrivelled hand to stand up and stretch it out (Mark 3:5).

The Old Testament is also full of symbolism and imagery of spiritual things. From a healing and wholeness perspective, there are numerous examples – there were the sacrifices for sin as part of the law in Leviticus 4 and the bronze snake on a pole so that anyone bitten by a snake infestation could look at it and live (Numbers 21). Elisha healed the army commander, Naaman, by telling him to wash in the river Jordan seven times (2 Kings 5) although, interestingly, he wasn't keen on the idea at first because it wasn't what he was expecting. And that, sometimes, is the nature of God's healing. We give ourselves up to his will but he doesn't always do what we expect.

> "I want to use the word Sacrament in its widest sense – an outward and visible sign bringing an inward blessing."
>
> Edgar Bell

The two main sacraments, where there is a lot of commonality and agreement between all mainstream church traditions, are baptism and communion. However, there is also a lot of disagreement – does

Day 1: Sacraments in healing – why bother?

the water and wine actually turn into Christ's body and blood or are they merely symbols of it? Should we be baptising infants or only adults? Should it be full immersion or is a sprinkling of water sufficient? We could go on. We are going to stick to areas of broad agreement and leave the more complex issues around theology to the theologians.

Fundamentally, the purpose of the sacraments is to bring us into and keep us in right relationship with God. They bring us into wholeness and help to try and keep us whole. It is therefore not surprising that when reading about people who have been healed, particularly in church traditions that place special value on the spiritual power of the sacraments, we find that they are often the source of power for healing and wholeness.

"For the purpose of the Sacraments is to initiate into, and to maintain the soul in perfect wholeness i.e. complete union with Christ."

Edgar Bell

Exercise:

Spend time thinking about and thanking God for the many different ways he heals.

Day 2: Initiating into wholeness: baptism and confirmation

"Or don't you know that all of us who were baptised into Christ Jesus were baptised into his death? We were therefore buried with him through baptism into death in order that, just as Christ was raised from the dead through the glory of the Father, we too may live a new life."

Romans 6:3-4

We are commanded in the Bible to be baptised as the first step on our Christian journey. After Saul encounters Jesus on the road to Damascus he loses his sight. This is restored by Ananias who tells him to respond to his calling by being baptised and calling on the name of Jesus (Acts 22:16).

At Pentecost, after the coming of the Holy Spirit as tongues of flame, Peter preaches to the crowds and urges those who want to accept the teaching to "Repent and be baptised, every one of you, in the name of Jesus Christ for the forgiveness of your sins. And you will receive the gift of the Holy Spirit" (Acts 2:38).

Baptism, therefore, brings us into healing and wholeness through a right relationship with God by spiritual cleansing and washing away our sin, as well as joining in Jesus' death and resurrection. It is the key response to hearing and accepting Jesus as our Saviour. It brings us into the family of God and makes us his child. We are signed, sealed and protected by him. It also brings us into the family of the church as part of the body of Christ. "For we were all baptised by one Spirit so as to form one body" (1 Corinthians 12:13).

Baptism links those powerful places of healing and wholeness – the foot of the cross of Jesus and the throne room of heaven. As 1 Peter 3:21-22 says, "This water symbolises baptism that now saves you also – not the removal of dirt from the body but the pledge of a clear conscience towards God. It saves you by the resurrection of Jesus Christ, who has gone into heaven and is at God's right hand – with angels, authorities and powers in submission to him."

Baptism is about dying and being reborn. It is spiritual death followed by spiritual life and is, perhaps, why physical death for Christians can be a form of healing. We are raised to new and eternal life in Jesus when we are baptised.

Baptism with water must be followed by baptism with the Holy Spirit, although this has sometimes already happened or happens at the point of being baptised with water. As we have seen already, the God who forgives our sin is also the God who gives us good things – firstly, our mentor, guide and helper, the Holy

Spirit. Both are necessary for our work in bringing in the kingdom of God through praying for healing and wholeness. As Jesus said, "Very truly I tell you, no one can enter the kingdom of God unless they are born of water and the Spirit" (John 3:5).

He commanded us to be baptised. "Then Jesus came to them and said, 'All authority in heaven and on earth has been given to me. Therefore go and make disciples of all nations, baptising them in the name of the Father and of the Son and of the Holy Spirit, and teaching them to obey everything I have commanded you'" (Matthew 28:18-20). It is therefore also an act of obedience.

> "The first great Sacrament of the Gospel initiates the soul into wholeness in Christ . . . [this] makes possible a new relationship to God. We are no longer outside the family of God, we have become sons [and daughters] of God and inheritors of the life eternal . . . What wonder is it therefore, if great blessings descend upon the person through this unique experience. Surely the marvel would be if nothing happened!"
>
> Edgar Bell

In some church traditions, the sacrament of baptism is linked to the sacrament of confirmation – where the promises made at the time of baptism (usually as a baby) are sealed or affirmed by the adult (or teenager). Confirmation usually also involves praying for the Holy Spirit and anointing with oil, which are part of healing and wholeness.

"It is difficult to assess the contribution made by Holy Confirmation towards wholeness. Its place in the Sacramental scheme is the completion of Holy Baptism and the doorway to Holy Communion, the second great Sacrament of the Gospel."

Edgar Bell

It is perhaps not surprising that some people receive the healing and wholeness they need at the point of baptism and/or confirmation. These acts of obedience can be powerful spiritually.

Exercise:

Read Isaiah 11:2. The Spirit that rested on Jesus is the same Spirit that we have asked for and will help us when we pray for healing for others. Spend time asking for an increasing amount of the qualities listed in the verse.

Day 3: Sustaining wholeness: Holy Communion

"For I received from the Lord what I also passed on to you: the Lord Jesus, on the night he was betrayed, took bread, and when he had given thanks, he broke it and said, 'This is my body, which is for you; do this in remembrance of me.' In the same way, after supper he took the cup, saying, 'This cup is the new covenant in my blood; do this, whenever you drink it, in remembrance of me.' For whenever you eat this bread and drink this cup, you proclaim the Lord's death until he comes."

1 Corinthians 11:23-26

Whether you call this sacrament the Eucharist, Holy Communion, Mass, the Lord's Supper or something else, all mainstream churches agree that the Bible commands that we commemorate the final supper Jesus had with his disciples because we are commanded to do so.

There is a warning in this passage that a failure to take this seriously may affect our health. It states, "Everyone ought to examine themselves before they eat of the bread and drink from the cup. For those who eat and drink without discerning the body of Christ eat and drink judgment on themselves. That is why many among you are weak and ill, and a number of you have fallen asleep" (1 Corinthians 11:28-30). This may sound harsh, but it comes within the context of this passage on abuses occurring at the Lord's Supper, including divisions between church members, and some people eating too much and getting drunk whilst others go hungry.

The commemoration of Jesus' death through celebration of the Lord's Supper brings us back in focus to the foot of the cross. It draws our attention to the last few hours of his life before the crucifixion and then the breaking of his body and the shedding of his blood at his death. It is, perhaps, no surprise then, that healing can occur powerfully and reasonably frequently at or after Christians celebrate this. Anything that brings Jesus' death so sharply back into focus and puts us firmly at the foot of the cross, is bound to have a powerful healing effect.

This also links to the passage where Jesus describes himself as the bread of life in saying, "I am the bread of life. Whoever comes to me will never go hungry, and whoever believes in me will never be thirsty" (John 6:35). He goes on to say, "I am the living bread that came down from heaven. Whoever eats this bread will live for ever. This bread is my flesh, which I will give for the life of the world . . . Very truly I tell you, unless you

Day 3: Sustaining wholeness: Holy Communion

eat the flesh of the Son of Man and drink his blood, you have no life in you. Whoever eats my flesh and drinks my blood has eternal life, and I will raise them up at the last day. For my flesh is real food and my blood is real drink. Whoever eats my flesh and drinks my blood remains in me, and I in them" (John 6:51, 53-56).

Here again we see a command to be obedient to sharing in the body and blood of Jesus. But there is a promise too – there is the promise of healing and wholeness and eternal life. Furthermore, the idea that communion helps us to "remain" in Jesus, strengthens the argument that this sacrament is one that maintains us in a state of wholeness.

> "We are on sure ground when we consider the place of Holy Communion in the Redemptive healing of Christ through His Church. For its purpose is to sustain and develop that Wholeness first granted to the soul through Holy Baptism."
>
> Edgar Bell

Exercise:

What do you think about when you are taking part in sharing the bread and wine in your tradition? Do you prepare for it? If so, how? Try and go to Communion or Mass (or however your tradition refers to this) and spend time reflecting on the potential spiritual power of what you are doing.

Day 4: Restoring wholeness: reconciliation and anointing of the sick

> "Therefore, if you are offering your gift at the altar and there remember that your brother or sister has something against you, leave your gift there in front of the altar. First go and be reconciled to them; then come and offer your gift."
>
> Matthew 5:23-24

Whether you call these practices sacraments or not, all mainstream churches agree with the need for the actions that constitute these sacraments.

The sacrament of reconciliation used to be called "penance" or "confession". It recognises that although we are forgiven at our baptism, we continue to sin and therefore need to have a way back into wholeness through repeated forgiveness. We need to be reconciled both to God and to each other as sin affects our relationships with other people as well as our relationship with our heavenly Father. This reconciliation restores us back into wholeness.

Today's verses from Matthew 5 reflect this. If we are coming to the altar and realise that there is something we need to sort out with someone else, we need to try and sort this out first and, where possible, reconcile to each other in order to be able to be reconciled to God.

Although confessing our sins to each other is not a feature of many protestant churches, it is recommended in the book of James, which says, "Therefore confess your sins to each other and pray for each other so that you may be healed" (James 5:16). Both Edgar Bell and Francis MacNutt describe powerful physical healings that occur when this happens.

Confession to each other means we need to have some assurance around consent, confidentiality and safeguarding, which we will look at next week.

The sacrament of the anointing of the sick is obviously connected with healing and wholeness. The history of it is perhaps a little interesting, in that it went through a period of being reserved for those who were dying until it was reclaimed in 1972 for those who were seriously ill. Interestingly, the Greek word for "mercy", *"Eleos"*, has the same root as the word for "oil".

In this practice, people who are sick are anointed with oil as well as being prayed for. There is a precedent for this in the gospels. For example, when Jesus sent out the twelve, we are told, "They drove out many demons and anointed with oil many people who were ill and healed them" (Mark 6:13).

I love the note in Francis MacNutt's book *Healing* which states, "In non-sacramental, Pentecostal churches, we also see a lively belief in the value of anointing with oil. I have met truck drivers who, with their little bottle of [blessed] oil . . . travel around anointing the sick and praying with them, faithfully following the example set by Jesus' first disciples."[7] I love this idea of ordinary people like you and me taking part in this!

This practice also occurs in obedience to the passage in James which states, "Is anyone among you ill? Let them call the elders of the church to pray over them and anoint them with oil in the name of the Lord. And the prayer offered in faith will make the sick person well; the Lord will raise them up. If they have sinned, they will be forgiven" (James 5:14-15). There are two different verbs being used here for making someone well and the Lord raising them up. Forgiveness is also included. So, the anointing with oil can have a powerful effect on all types of healing needed for restoration of wholeness.

> "Amongst the lesser Sacraments are two which are primarily concerned with restoration to wholeness when there has been a falling away either through sin or through sickness. The first of these is the Sacrament of Penance or Absolution, the purpose

---

7. Francis MacNutt, *Healing* (Notre Dame, Indiana: Ave Maria Press, 1999).

of which is to bring to pass the restoration of the soul after a spiritual lapse. When a person is sick in body or mind, the cause is often to be found in the soul's deep need to unburden sin and eliminate the sense of guilt . . . The other Sacrament [Holy Unction] concerned with restoration starts from the opposite angle, i.e. with the body and mind – and leads on to the renewal of the entire person."

Edgar Bell

Exercise:

Are there people in your life, either now or in the past, who you have struggled to forgive and be reconciled to? Bring these challenging situations to God today.

Day 5: Other sacraments

"And you, my son Solomon, acknowledge the God of your father, and serve him with wholehearted devotion and with a willing mind, for the Lord searches every heart and understands every desire and every thought. If you seek him, he will be found by you; but if you forsake him, he will reject you for ever. Consider now, for the Lord has chosen you to build a house as the sanctuary. Be strong and do the work."

1 Chronicles 28:9-10

The sacraments, like the rest of healing and wholeness, sit in a context of service, devotion, willingness, honesty, persistence and obedience. This is all reflected in David's advice to his son, Solomon, at the end of his reign and is good advice for us too.

The final two sacraments, which don't affect all of us but are relevant in special circumstances, are those of marriage and ordination.

Marriage

The processes around healing and wholeness bring us into right relationship with God and right relationships with each other. Good relationships keep us healthy. So, it's perhaps not surprising that Francis MacNutt has found physical healing occurring, almost as a by-product, during processes around counselling and prayer for healing of marital relationships.

Christian marriage envisages Christ at the centre of the relationship – the third strand in a cord: "Though one may be overpowered, two can defend themselves. A cord of three strands is not quickly broken" (Ecclesiastes 4:12).

However, not all are called to marriage. Many are called to singleness. The importance here is about right relationships both with each other and with God. I would argue that the sacrament of marriage which occurs in some church traditions is a part of this.

"Where two persons so joined together find their unity in Christ, the greatest possible blessedness and happiness follows . . . Happiness is one of the greatest sources of health and often it makes it possible for both partners to triumph gloriously over poverty, disappointment and sickness, because the crosses of this life are brought, in fellowship, into union with the Sacrifice of Christ."

Edgar Bell

Ordination

Ordination, or the sacrament of Holy Orders, occurs when ordinary people are called and trained into leadership with a church. There is usually a process involving the laying on of hands and often anointing with oil within churches that commissions an individual to the work he or she is called to. This is consistent with the example of Jesus. We are told, "You know what has happened throughout the province of Judea, beginning in Galilee after the baptism that John preached – how God anointed Jesus of Nazareth with the Holy Spirit and power, and how he went around doing good and healing all who were under the power of the devil, because God was with him" (Acts 10:37-38). He was anointed by God and into service.

Similarly, the seven chosen to "wait on tables" in Acts 6 were commissioned by the apostles: "They presented these men to the apostles, who prayed and laid their hands on them" (Acts 6:6).

Finally, Timothy was told, "Command and teach these things. Don't let anyone look down on you because you are young, but set an example for the believers in speech, in conduct, in love, in faith and in purity. Until I come, devote yourself to the public reading of Scripture, to preaching and to teaching. Do not neglect your gift, which was given you through prophecy when the body of elders laid their hands on you. Be diligent in these matters; give yourself wholly to them, so that everyone may see your progress. Watch your life and doctrine closely. Persevere in them, because if you do, you will save both yourself and your hearers" (1 Timothy 4:11-16). Note that he was granted the gifting he needed for the service of God at the time the body of elders laid hands on him.

It should therefore not be surprising that we hear of people receiving healing, wholeness and gifting at the instance of ordination.

> "Who can estimate the extent of the power, strength, the wisdom, granted through this Sacrament? Many a priest, aware of his inadequacy of the task he has undertaken find that the grace of God is indeed sufficient."
>
> Edgar Bell

Exercise:

One thing we discover when thinking about healing and wholeness is that physical healing is wrapped up with healing of the past, memories, spiritual sickness and relationships with God and with others. Think about your close friends and family and pray that God will bless, strengthen and renew those relationships.

Day 6: Reasons why people aren't physically healed

"We know that the whole creation has been groaning as in the pains of childbirth right up to the present time. Not only so, but we ourselves, who have the firstfruits of the Spirit, groan inwardly as we wait eagerly for our adoption to sonship, the redemption of our bodies. For in this hope we were saved. But hope that is seen is no hope at all. Who hopes for what they already have? But if we hope for what we do not yet have, we wait for it patiently. In the same way, the Spirit helps us in our weakness. We do not know what we ought to pray for, but the Spirit himself intercedes for us through wordless groans. And he who searches our hearts knows the mind of the Spirit, because the Spirit intercedes for God's people in accordance with the will of God."

Romans 8:22-27

As part of the mentoring or debriefing, you may wish to think about other reasons people are not physically healed. We have already thought about spiritual battles and the kingdom and will of God. The below are detailed by Francis MacNutt in his book *Healing*. He lists twelve reasons why people aren't healed but suggests there may be more:

1. Lack of faith – in a God who loves us, died to save us, continues to intercede for us and wants to heal us.

2. Redemptive suffering – I don't think for a moment that God wills people to suffer, but as we have seen, it happens and, very occasionally, God can and does use physical illness for a higher purpose. For example, in Galatians 4:13 Paul writes, "As you know, it was because of an illness that I first preached the gospel to you."

3. A false value attached to suffering – redemptive suffering is rare. But it doesn't stop people sometimes feeling guilty for asking God to take away their illness. Sometimes they feel that God has given it to them for a reason and they feel guilty if they ask for it to be removed.

4. Sin – we have already seen that sometimes forgiveness needs to come first before any physical healing can take place.

5. Not praying specifically – this is about getting to the root of the problem. Sometimes there is a specific experience or memory which needs to be addressed and dealt with before healing can occur. Words of knowledge can be really

helpful here in pointing to where the problem is. Sometimes, people need counselling as part of prayer.

6. Faulty diagnosis – for example, praying for physical healing when forgiveness or healing from previous abuse is what is needed.

7. Refusal to see medicine as a way God heals – God uses doctors and medicine for healing as we have seen.

8. Not using the natural means of preserving health – as Francis MacNutt writes, "If you eat junk food, if you smoke, if you don't exercise, you should not always expect that prayer will compensate for the lack of discipline that has led to your sickliness."[8]

9. Now is not the time – when healing occurs in relation to prayer and the speed at which is does can be totally unpredictable. God sometimes heals immediately, sometimes gradually, sometimes within minutes and sometimes years later.

10. A different person is required to pray – sometimes God uses someone else to accomplish the task of healing we have started. The most common story I hear is of persistent prayer by the family of a sick person when nothing seems to happen. Then someone totally unconnected to the family prays for that person and healing happens.

---

8. This quote implies that illness can be caused by self-indulgence – which it can – but we also know that there are wider determinants for these behaviours which may need to be addressed.

11. Demonic interference – this can occur particularly if someone has been involved in the occult. We've seen the story in Daniel of demonic inference in spiritual response.

12. Wrong social environment – for example, sometimes illness results from poor relationships and so sometimes the healing of the relationships needs to come first. I would also argue that this covers the anxiety of family members, which seems to sometimes impede healing, as we have seen. It is notable that Jesus often deals with the family first before he heals the person. For example, he ministers to Martha and Mary first, before raising Lazarus from the dead (John 11) and gets further information from and deals with the issue of belief with the father, before healing the child in Mark 9.

There are other reasons too, as we have already seen. I would argue the following:

13. We have stopped praying too soon. We give up too easily. We aren't persistent and faithful in our devotion to prayer for someone.

14. We miss the opportunity of healing through the sacraments because we don't take them seriously enough.

In these cases, we need to throw ourselves and those who we pray for at the feet of Jesus and ask the Holy Spirit for his intercession on our behalf.

> **Exercise:**
>
> Spend time going through the list from today. Have you prayed for people for healing in the past where one of the above may have applied?

Day 7: Reflection

It's time to rest, relax and reflect.

> "Blessed are those whose strength is in you,
> whose hearts are set on pilgrimage.
> As they pass through the Valley of Baka,
> they make it a place of springs;
> the autumn rains also cover it with pools.
> They go from strength to strength,
> till each appears before God in Zion."
>
> (Psalm 84:5-7)

The "Valley of Baka" can be translated as "the valley of weeping". Bring to God your church or organisation and pray that it too will result in weeping turning into springs of life and refreshment.

Week 5: Group discussion questions

The list of questions below are suggestions only. The group may have other areas they wish to explore. Encourage group members to discuss and reflect on their experiences.

1. How have you found this week? Was there anything that surprised or struck you? Was there anything new or different? Is there anything that you didn't understand or disagreed with?

2. What is the role of sacraments in your church tradition? How are they used? Is there a link to healing and wholeness in the way they are celebrated? Of the sacraments described, which do you think are the most important for healing and wholeness?

3. Are you aware of any instances in your own experience of healing and wholeness occurring through receiving a sacrament? What has been your experience of baptism and (if appropriate to your tradition) confirmation?

4. How often is Holy Communion celebrated in your church? What are your expectations of this when you receive it?

5. What does the group think about confessing sin to each other? How about anointing with oil?
6. Does your church ever do services of healing? Is there a place for this? Can these be linked to evangelism and outreach?
7. Is there a link between evangelism and healing? If so, what is it?

As a group, read through the list of reasons why people aren't physically healed from Day 6. Is there anything here which is new or surprising to you? Is there anything here that might change how you pray for people who are sick?

Week 6:

What else does my church/ organisation need to consider?

Well – you are almost at the end of this six-week Bible study in healing and wholeness. We have looked at whether God cares, why physical healing doesn't always happen, sought to understand spiritual battles and got into spiritual exercises with taking people we pray for to the foot of the cross or the throne room of God.

Then we have looked at the practical aspects of praying for someone, the need for a prayer buddy, for rest, for spiritual washing, for mentoring, for integration. We've also taken a look at sacraments and their role in healing and wholeness.

In this final section, we are going to take a look at how this – how you as you pray for others – fits into the fellowship you are a part of, and the wider mission and ministry of the church in all its forms.

Day 1: Healing and wholeness within the church context

"The man brought me back to the entrance to the temple, and I saw water coming out from under the threshold of the temple towards the east (for the temple faced east). The water was coming down from under the south side of the temple, south of the altar. He then brought me out through the north gate and led me around the outside to the outer gate facing east, and the water was trickling from the south side . . . Swarms of living creatures will live wherever the river flows. There will be large numbers of fish, because this water flows there and makes the salt water fresh; so where the river flows everything will live. Fishermen will stand along the shore; from En Gedi to En Eglaim there will be places for spreading nets. The fish will be of many kinds – like the fish of the Mediterranean Sea . . . Fruit trees of all kinds will grow on both banks of the river. Their leaves will not wither, nor will their fruit fail. Every month they will bear fruit, because the water from the sanctuary flows to them. Their fruit will serve for food and their leaves for healing."

Ezekiel 47:1-2, 9-10, 12

In the book of Ezekiel, the final vision (which encompasses chapters 40 to 48) is of a new temple and a new land. He was writing in a time after the destruction of Jerusalem and the original temple, and the vision is a mix of the practical, the apocalyptic and the symbolic. I want to use this passage to suggest that the temple, or today's church, can have an impact on the surrounding community through the outpouring of God's love and power, which the church itself cannot contain and so floods out into the land beyond, leading to peace, prosperity and healing in the surrounding community.

As communities of Christians, this is what we want to achieve. That our buildings and communities become so full of God's love and power that it floods out and impacts onto the people and land surrounding us.

We see in Acts 2 that after the coming of the Holy Spirit at Pentecost, many of the crowd believed and were baptised, which included three thousand on one day. We are told, "They devoted themselves to the apostles' teaching and to fellowship, to the breaking of bread and to prayer. Everyone was filled with awe at the many wonders and signs performed by the apostles. All the believers were together and had everything in

Day 1: Healing and wholeness within the church context

common. They sold property and possessions to give to anyone who had need. Every day they continued to meet together in the temple courts. They broke bread in their homes and ate together with glad and sincere hearts, praising God and enjoying the favour of all the people. And the Lord added to their number daily those who were being saved" (Acts 2:42-47).

This is how the earliest church responded to an outpouring of the Holy Spirit. They broke bread (communion), they devoted themselves to teaching and to fellowship. They devoted themselves to prayer. They sold property and possessions. They gave to those in need. They ate together with glad and sincere hearts. They praised God. They enjoyed favour of all people. They grew in number.

We have already seen that when Jesus sent out the twelve into the surrounding land and villages "he gave them power and authority to drive out all demons and to cure diseases, and he sent them out to proclaim the kingdom of God and to heal those who were ill" (Luke 9:1-2). Then, when he sent out the seventy-two ordinary people like us to the local communities, he commanded them to "heal those there who are ill and tell them, 'The kingdom of God has come near to you'" (Luke 10:9).

Prayer for healing and wholeness is, therefore, part of the service that Christian communities should be offering to those around them. It's not to be kept to ourselves – we have a powerful God who loves to touch those in need.

Exercise:

Think about how your church or organisation shows love to the surrounding community both locally but also further afield. What stops it happening even more powerfully? Pray through any issues you think of.

Day 2: Consent, confidentiality and safeguarding

"A new command I give you: love one another. As I have loved you, so you must love one another. By this everyone will know that you are my disciples, if you love one another."

John 13:34-35

There are three areas of ethics and law that we need to be aware of when we start praying for people. I see adhering to these as love in action.

The first is *consent*. We usually wait for people to ask for prayer. As we have seen, Jesus responded to those who asked, he didn't force it on people who didn't. Those being prayed for need to consent to the way we are praying for them and be comfortable with it. You need to ask their consent before, for example, placing a hand on their shoulder. When you are praying with someone, they can withdraw their consent for you to pray for them or to touch them whilst praying, at any time and without giving you a reason why. If they wish to leave, they can just do so and you cannot stop them.

You must not try to coerce someone into having prayer or being prayed with in a way you want, or to continue praying without their permission. This may stop us praying *with* someone; it doesn't stop us praying *for* someone. If we are sitting on a bus and see someone through the window sitting on the pavement and struggling with life, we can pray silently for them without their consent. If we are going to leap off the bus, run to them and offer to lay hands of them, anoint them with oil and pray, we will need their consent.

The second area of ethics and law is *confidentiality*. When people come forward for prayer, they may tell us things that are confidential and trust us to keep their secret. They may tell us because of the need to confess sin, or because something appalling has happened to them in the past that they need to speak about in order to access healing and restoration from God. It is your duty as their supporter and helper in the healing journey to keep confidential things confidential, unless something illegal is disclosed or where someone is at risk of harm. Prayer ministry is dependent on a relationship of trust. The person being prayed for is trusting the people doing the praying to do it in a way that maintains their dignity and privacy. We have a duty of care to those asking for prayer to ensure this happens.

Finally, there is the issue of *safeguarding*. The organisation Baptists Together states, "Safeguarding is the protection of adults and children from harm, abuse or neglect. We all have the same rights and expectations to independence, respect, choice, fulfilment of our ambitions, to be heard, included, and to have privacy and confidentiality."[9]

The Church of England states, "Safeguarding means the action the Church takes to promote a safer culture. This means we will promote the welfare of children, young people and adults, work to prevent abuse from occurring, seek to protect those that are at risk of being abused and respond well to those that have been abused."[10]

A number of denominations have produced safeguarding standards, including the Catholic Church which, in the UK, has eight national safeguarding standards.[11]

When people come to ask for prayer for healing, they may disclose issues around abuse. They may have been abused by others or they may have been the abuser. Abuse can be physical, emotional, sexual, spiritual or neglect. This may be historic or it may be an ongoing issue. Abuse needs to be dealt with for the purposes of wholeness. However, if something is disclosed which means that someone is at risk of harm, you may need to break confidentiality in order to safeguard the person or people involved. So, before you start, make sure you have access to your organisation's safeguarding

---

9. Baptist Union of Great Britain (2021), "Introduction to Safeguarding Support for Baptist Churches", https://www.baptist.org.uk/Publisher/File.aspx?ID=279610 (accessed July 2024).
10. Church of England (2017), "Promoting a Safer Church", https://www.churchofengland.org/sites/default/files/2017-11/promoting-a-safer-church-policy-notes.pdf (accessed July 2024).
11. Catholic Safeguarding Standards Agency (2020), "The Eight National Safeguarding Standards", https://catholicsafeguarding.org.uk/resources/the-eight-national-safeguarding-standards/ (accessed July 2024).

policy, you know who the safeguarding leads are and you know who you will turn to for advice if faced with a difficult safeguarding situation.

Exercise:

Ask God to open your eyes to issues of risk and safety, and to increase your awareness of issues related to consent, confidentiality and safeguarding.

Then, why not do a practical task? Find, read through and pray about your organisation's safeguarding policy. Try and find some safeguarding training, preferably one that is Christian and includes discussing spiritual abuse.

Day 3: Managing risk

"Be alert and of sober mind. Your enemy the devil prowls around like a roaring lion looking for someone to devour."

1 Peter 5:8

There is no doubt that people have come to harm in the past from very well-intentioned prayer for healing. For example, people where prayer has been used in a coercive way, along with spiritual threats of hell and damnation, for those who have sought help and healing around issues of sexual orientation and attraction.

Like all risk, we need to understand what risks we run to be able to manage them effectively. Let's look at them from several different perspectives.

Firstly, there is the risk to those asking for prayer. When people come asking for prayer for healing, they can be very vulnerable. It takes courage to ask for prayer and they may be fearful of what may (or may not) happen. If, when we pray for them, we uncover deep dark issues, they become even more vulnerable. Sometimes, it is those who are most vulnerable in society who ask for prayer. Vulnerable people are at high risk of harm if they are not cared for well. The risks are spiritual, physical, emotional and psychological. We must be sensible, kind and loving.

Be careful where you put your hands and where they move to during prayer! Avoid stroking and cuddling. Be gentle but professional. We must keep people safe as we journey with them. Whether we take them to the foot of the cross, into the throne room of God or ask Jesus to come into the room and take over, we must stay with them and protect them until they are safe in the hands of their heavenly Father.

Secondly, there are risks to those doing the praying. There are spiritual risks we run when we engage in spiritual battles during prayer, as we have already seen. We need to be spiritually washed off and debriefed afterwards with someone who is in a training or mentoring capacity for us. There are other risks around safeguarding and vulnerability. Praying in twos – having a prayer buddy – means that you are able to chaperone each other during a time when you are dealing with a vulnerable person.

> "The minister of healing may run serious spiritual risks if he acts alone."
> Edgar Bell

Avoid praying one-on-one in a closed room on your own, particularly if you are praying for a member of the opposite sex. You may end up later with unwanted allegations about what happened and you may struggle to defend them. There is nothing scary about this but you must be sensible and pragmatic. Pray in twos. Keep the door open. Make sure there are others around who can keep an eye on what's happening if you aren't working as part of a bigger team. Yes, you have a duty to care for the one you are praying for but you need to keep yourself safe too.

Thirdly, there is the risk to the reputation of the organisation you are representing if you get prayer ministry wrong. No organisation wants to be at the centre of a social media or tabloid newspaper storm with accusations, for example, of groping during prayer, inappropriate conduct or safeguarding. Stay safe, be sensible and remember, these are spiritual battles and so we must expect that the devil may get annoyed with us and try to undermine what we are trying to do. Pray for protection for the prayer ministry team, if you have one, or at least all those involved in praying for others.

> "After all, the dear Lord Himself never acted alone. He gathered around Him a group of chosen men, and trained them to observe, and later to do, what he did."
>
> Edgar Bell

Exercise:

Think through and then pray through how your organisation manages risk. Is there anything else that the leadership should consider?

Day 4: Oversight, governance, training and accountability

"To the elders among you, I appeal as a fellow elder and a witness of Christ's sufferings who also will share in the glory to be revealed: be shepherds of God's flock that is under your care, watching over them – not because you must, but because you are willing, as God wants you to be; not pursuing dishonest gain, but eager to serve; not lording it over those entrusted to you, but being examples to the flock."

1 Peter 5:1-3

In my opinion, any organisation that runs a group of people dedicated to praying with others, needs to have some thought put into their oversight, governance, accountability and training. We are going to be held to account by God in due course but we need to be held to account by each other now. Hebrews 4 states, "For the word of God is alive and active. Sharper than any double-edged sword, it penetrates even to dividing soul and spirit, joints and marrow; it judges the thoughts and attitudes of the heart. Nothing in all creation is hidden from God's sight. Everything is uncovered and laid bare before the eyes of him to whom we must give account" (Hebrews 4:12-13).

The passage on the body of Christ (1 Corinthians 12:12-27) reminds us that what affects one of us will affect us all. If one of our fellowship is hurting or broken, then, like a broken wrist, it will affect the rest of the body from properly functioning. We cannot win races if part of us is broken.

Prayer for healing and wholeness needs to happen within the context of Christian community and, for the reasons described in the last two days, needs to have governance around it. I would suggest the following:

1. There is someone with responsibility for prayer ministry within the leadership of the organisation. They need to be familiar with the ethics and law related to praying for others as well as the risks that can be encountered. Ideally, they should be someone with an interest and experience in praying for healing and wholeness for others, but I personally don't think this is mandatory – someone spiritual and sensible sitting within the church leadership will do an excellent job anyway.

2. There needs to be appropriate policies in place, particularly a safeguarding policy and nominated safeguarding leads. These need to be discussed and documented as being approved by the leadership council within the organisation.

3. There probably should be some sort of documented formal existence of the prayer team and some sort of regular reporting back into the church leadership council, which should be documented.

4. Whenever prayer for healing happens, there should be someone experienced nominated as the person who debriefs, mentors and supports the others. It may be that this person does not, themselves, take part in the praying but supports and mentors the other members of the team that they are training.

5. There should be formal training which covers all the practical and spiritual aspects of praying for others in order to build a team and build experience. We also need practice, practice, practice – we are all called but some are gifted and, in any case, we all need practice to develop whatever gifts and skills we have been given.

All of these activities themselves need to be covered in prayer. We do these things because we wish to participate in God's ministry – it is his, not ours. But we need to build a framework which allows us to do this safely within the environments we pray and worship in.

> "There are serious dangers to be guarded against ... and no one person, however advanced he may be in the spiritual life, can be certain of being able to face such dangers in isolation. They should be met in Fellowship."
>
> Edgar Bell

Finally, your organisation may wish to consider other aspects of prayer for healing and wholeness. Is there a need for a regular service of healing, perhaps yearly? How can persistent prayer for individuals be sustained? Is there a need for an intercessory prayer group? How about a soaking prayer room? How do we, as a group, keep up endurance and sustainability in prayer for healing and wholeness? How about lists or diaries of prayers and answers? A twenty-four-hour prayer place perhaps? Different organisations will have different ideas as to how to do this.

Exercise:

Next time you are in the building of your organisation or church, quietly prayer-walk it, asking God to fill every space with his presence, his power and his love. (Prayer-walking is where you walk around something praying for it as you go. It can be done silently on your own, or out loud with someone else as if having a conversation.)

Day 5: Group preparation

"At the time of sacrifice, the prophet Elijah stepped forward and prayed: 'Lord, the God of Abraham, Isaac and Israel, let it be known today that you are God in Israel and that I am your servant and have done all these things at your command. Answer me, Lord, answer me, so these people will know that you, Lord, are God, and that you are turning their hearts back again.' Then the fire of the Lord fell and burned up the sacrifice, the wood, the stones and the soil, and also licked up the water in the trench."

1 Kings 18:36-38

We have already discussed deep personal preparation for praying for others and the importance of this. Although I am keen to avoid any suggestion of formulas when it comes to physical healing, it is wise to adopt good practice and it does seem that sometimes the greater the preparation, the greater the outpouring of the Holy Spirit for healing. In any case, what have we got to lose by preparing thoroughly?

We have seen how we do this as individuals. Let's think about what we do as a group. Both are important. First, let's look at some biblical examples of preparation.

Just before his arrest, trial and crucifixion, Jesus spent time preparing in the garden of Gethsemane. He took three others with him – Peter, James and John – who were instructed to "watch and pray" (Matthew 26:41). We are told of his anguish and how he felt overwhelmed. The version in Luke tells us, "And being in anguish, he prayed more earnestly, and his sweat was like drops of blood falling to the ground" (Luke 22:44). If Jesus took serious time to struggle with God about an issue of suffering and pain and prepare himself for what was coming, how much more should we?

Elijah, as we have already seen, was a man capable of sustained and fervent prayer. How do you think he prepared for his encounter with the prophets of Baal on Mount Carmel in 1 Kings 18?

Esther, on learning of Haman's plot to kill the Jews, said to her uncle Mordecai, "Go, gather together all the Jews who are in Susa, and fast for me. Do not eat or drink for three days, night or day. I and my attendants will fast as you do. When this is done, I will go to the king, even though it is against the law. And if I perish, I perish" (Esther 4:16).

Daniel, again a man of prayer and preparation, also got others to pray. We are told, "At this, Daniel went in to the king and asked for time, so that he might interpret the dream for him. Then Daniel returned to his house and explained the matter to his friends Hananiah, Mishael and Azariah. He urged them to plead for mercy from the God of heaven concerning this mystery, so that he and his friends might not be executed with the rest of the wise men of Babylon. During the night the mystery was revealed to Daniel in a vision" (Daniel 2:16-19).

So, if we are planning to offer the chance for people to come for prayer for healing and wholeness, perhaps following a meeting or service, how do we as a group pray? I would suggest the following:

1. Personal preparation, as we have seen in Week 3, Day 1: "Be whole".
2. Spend time praying for each other, for healing and wholeness within the group, for the Holy Spirit to be on each member of the group to guard them and guide them, speak clearly to them and give them wisdom. Ask for gifting or an increase in gifting for the purposes of service to others.
3. Pray for all those who will be coming to the gathering, meeting or service – whatever it is. Perhaps stand by the door and greet them and pray silently for them as they come in.
4. Pray for those who will be asking for prayer.
5. Prayer-walk the venue – simply walk around the physical space all of this is happening in and pray for God to be present, powerful and active. I suggest doing this in twos.

6. If the leadership of the meeting is uncomfortable, pray as a group for words of knowledge that can be given out.

Finally, don't give up! I was struck when reading John Wimber's book *Power Healing*, how, despite the fact he had a powerful special gift for healing, there was a period of months at the start of his ministry where he prayed for numerous people and nothing happened. Keep going! Many of us do not have a powerful gift for healing, but this is God's ministry and he will use us if we are willing.

> **Exercise:**
>
> If you are in a group of people who pray together for others, think about how you prepare. Is there more you could be doing? Ask God to give you wisdom as to how to do this well.

Day 6: Sharing answers to prayer

"Then Peter said, 'Silver or gold I do not have, but what I do have I give you. In the name of Jesus Christ of Nazareth, walk.' Taking him by the right hand, he helped him up, and instantly the man's feet and ankles became strong. He jumped to his feet and began to walk. Then he went with them into the temple courts, walking and jumping, and praising God. When all the people saw him walking and praising God, they recognised him as the same man who used to sit begging at the temple gate called Beautiful, and they were filled with wonder and amazement at what had happened to him."

Acts 3:6-10

As we have already seen, the purposes of healing are to bring glory to God and usually results in people being brought into service, or further into service, for him. In this passage from Acts 3, the immediate reaction to instantaneous physical healing was to praise God and it resulted in those around him being filled with wonder and amazement. We have also already seen the importance of thankfulness following healing.

Within Christian circles, physical healing can build faith. We say we believe in an all-powerful God who can and does do miraculous things, but our belief is strengthened when we see and hear examples of it, particularly from within our own community and of people we know. It is really important, therefore, that where possible we encourage each other with sharing answers to prayer, no matter how small or large that prayer was or the answer is. How you, your church or organisation or home group do this will vary but needs to be considered.

Worship as a response to the power and love of Jesus can take different forms. For example, in one story we are told, "Six days before the Passover, Jesus came to Bethany, where Lazarus lived, whom Jesus had raised from the dead. Here a dinner was given in Jesus' honour. Martha served, while Lazarus was among those reclining at the table with him. Then Mary took about half a litre of pure nard, an expensive perfume; she poured it on Jesus' feet and wiped his feet with her hair. And the house was filled with the fragrance of the perfume" (John 12:1-3). Although commentators don't fully agree on who this Mary was, one view is that this was Mary, the sibling of Martha. It is therefore possible that the extravagant act of worship and devotion recorded in John 12 is in response to the raising of Lazarus from the dead, described in John 11. If this was the case, it wasn't a spontaneous immediate act of praise to God, but a deliberate, prepared, planned act of extravagant giving and worship of God in response to an amazing outpouring of his love and power.

It is also worth noting that in Acts 2, the number of believers grew quickly with the demonstration of miraculous signs and wonders with many being baptised. Furthermore, we are told, "But if an unbeliever or an inquirer comes in while everyone is prophesying, they are convicted of sin and are brought under judgment by all, as the secrets of their hearts are laid bare. So they will fall down and worship God, exclaiming, 'God is really among you!'" (1 Corinthians 14:24-25). However, miraculous signs also sometimes resulted in fear, scepticism, anger and opposition to those outside the community of believers in the Bible.

Finally, although worship, praise, thankfulness and devotion to the service of God is the usual and right response to the demonstration of the power and love of God, it sometimes is the vehicle for it. Sometimes God responds to our worship by an act of power and love.

One example of this is the story from 2 Chronicles 20 where we are told, "After consulting the people, Jehoshaphat appointed men to sing to the LORD and to praise him for the splendour of his holiness as they went out at the head of the army, saying: 'Give thanks to the LORD, for his love endures for ever.' As they began to sing and praise, the LORD set ambushes against the men of Ammon and Moab and Mount Seir who were invading Judah, and they were defeated" (2 Chronicles 20:21-22).

We are also told to "Ascribe to the LORD the glory due his name; bring an offering and come before him. Worship the LORD in the splendour of his holiness" (1 Chronicles 16:29).

> ## Exercise:
>
> "I waited patiently for the LORD; he turned to me and heard my cry. He lifted me out of the slimy pit, out of the mud and mire; he set my feet on a rock and gave me a firm place to stand. He put a new song in my mouth, a hymn of praise to our God. Many will see and fear the LORD and put their trust in him" (Psalm 40:1-3).
>
> Spend time thinking through these verses today and reflecting on them.

Day 7: Reflection

It's time to rest, relax and reflect.

As we come to the end of this journey, pray this prayer today:

> "For this reason I kneel before the Father, from whom every family in heaven and on earth derives its name. I pray that out of his glorious riches he may strengthen you with power through his Spirit in your inner being, so that Christ may dwell in your hearts through faith. And I pray that you, being rooted and established in love, may have power, together with all the Lord's holy people, to grasp how wide and long and high and deep is the love of Christ, and to know this love that surpasses knowledge – that you may be filled to the measure of all the fullness of God. Now to him who is able to do immeasurably more than all we ask or imagine, according to his power that is at work within us, to him be glory in the church and in Christ Jesus throughout all generations, for ever and ever! Amen."
>
> (Ephesians 3:14-21)

Week 6: Group discussion questions

The list of questions below are suggestions only. The group may have other areas they wish to explore. Encourage group members to discuss and reflect on their experiences.

1. How have you found this week? Was there anything that surprised or struck you? Was there anything new or different? Is there anything that you didn't understand or disagreed with?

2. How do you think prayer for healing and wholeness lead to blessing to the surrounding community? With so many people in our local areas struggling with issues of unwholeness, how can we reach out to them?

3. What are the problems that could arise if people pray for others without consideration of:

    a. Consent?
    b. Confidentiality?
    c. Safeguarding?

4. How easy do you find it to keep things others tell you confidential? Where do the tensions arise between confidentiality and

safeguarding? How would you manage someone who disclosed something during prayer which was illegal or suggested that someone else was at risk of harm?

5. What spiritual risks do we run when we engage in prayer with others for healing and wholeness? How can we protect ourselves and mitigate these risks? What risks may those coming forward for prayer be taking? How can we keep them safe?

6. What does your church/organisation have with respect to the following to support those praying for others for healing and wholeness?

    a. Policies
    b. Training and mentoring
    c. Support
    d. Debriefing
    e. Oversight and accountability

7. If you are involved in a group that contributes to a church or Christian organisation activity, how do you prepare for the activity? Is prayer a part of this?

As a group, prayerfully think about in what ways your church/organisation is a safe place for those seeking prayer for healing and wholeness as well as those doing the praying. What works well? Is there anything that could or should be done differently? Bring the things you think about and discuss to God in prayer.

Part 3

Appendices

Appendix A: A note to those in the healing professions

When I first started taking prayer for healing and wholeness for others seriously, I began to realise that a great divide had appeared in my life. I would go to work where I would spend time talking to people about their physical symptoms, examining them, arranging investigations, performing endoscopy procedures and surgical procedures, all within a secular framework and environment. God doesn't usually come into the conversation as a medical professional. On the other hand, out of work I'd spend time thinking about and praying for and with people to be made whole and be healed.

How, then, do we marry these areas of healing and wholeness within our professional lives, where we generally cannot obviously lay hands on people and ask for the Holy Spirit to fill them, with what we do outside of paid employment?

I use the term "healing professions" in the widest sense – we have seen how healing and wholeness encompasses mental, emotional and spiritual health, and how "illness" in our past, painful memories, damaging relationships past or present can impact on our overall health. So any profession that helps people to become more whole in any aspect, could be considered a healing profession.

I have come to believe that we, working within a healing profession for a secular employer, have a special obligation and ministry to those who we serve and care for professionally. We may be the only people who ever pray for some of the people we look after. We may be the only people who pray for the Holy Spirit to come on those we will care for that day. We are usually not in a position to pray with people professionally but there is nothing to stop us praying for them. And not just them. Patients sit within wider networks of family and friends. The health and wellbeing of one person in that network affects the rest. So pray also for the close friends and family of the person you are caring for. You may be the only person who ever does. Love them well.

Here are a few things I try and do regularly:

- When I have a clinic, I try and get there early. I close the door and try and spend some uninterrupted time in prayer. I ask the Holy Spirit to fill the room. I try and place my clinic room at the foot of the cross in my mind, so that anyone walking through the door is brought close to a Jesus who loved them, died for them and intercedes for them. I pray for God's wisdom that I won't miss anything and that I'll make the right set of decisions for each person who comes in. I pray that God will help me build relationship and open my eyes and ears to the non-physical aspects of illness that are important and I might need to address as part of treating them. Finally, I pray for the staff I'm working with and the others who will use the room. I sit and listen in God's presence.

- When I am examining someone, either in clinic or on the ward, I again ask God to use my hands (and my eyes and ears) for the benefit of that person. I ask that I will not miss anything and that I will accurately pick up anything I need to.

- When I scrub for an operation, I pray that God will help me do the very best I can for that patient. I pray that he will anoint my hands for the healing work they are about to undertake. Again, help me not to do anything stupid, or miss anything important.

- I pray for my patients and their families on the ward. I will admit that the patient who has major surgery or suffers a complication does get far more prayer than the person who comes in for a minor procedure, but I try and make sure that somehow, I have sought wholeness in everyone I am trying to administer physical healing to.

- Finally, I name my colleagues before God and pray for them. God told those in exile in Jeremiah 29:7 to "Also, seek the peace and prosperity of the city to which I have carried you into exile. Pray to the LORD for it, because if it prospers, you too will prosper". We aren't obviously in exile in our daily work, but I would suggest we should follow the same principle – to pray to God for our workplaces, colleagues and leadership teams.

In Ecclesiastes we are told, "Whatever your hand finds to do, do it with all your might" (Ecclesiastes 9:10). So, wherever you are and whatever you're doing, do it as if working for God, the only person to whom you are ultimately accountable.

As my great-grandfather Edgar Bell says, *"Finally, I am confident of this, that complete healing – the wholeness of which I have spoken – is most likely to be achieved if the members of the Medical Profession (Doctors, Nurses and their innumerable helpers and co-operators) are Christian men and women, who have surrendered themselves to Christ, and are ready to make a similar kind of preparation, according to need and opportunity, as I have described . . . They must get rid of self, become humble servants of Christ, and so be used to bring restoration not merely to that level of health from which their patient has departed, but to a new level of wholeness . . . Priest, Patient, Parents, Practitioners all surrendered to Christ! Surely!"*

Appendix B: Sermon suggestions

Here are a few thoughts for those in leadership positions who want to teach on healing and wholeness within their church/organisation.

Sermon 1: Healing and wholeness – what are we trying to achieve when we pray?

Suggested passage: Mark 2:1-12 – the healing of the paralysed man.

- God forgives the man's sin first and heals his body later. He is more interested in wholeness than just physical healing. His priority here was to forgive the man his sin. Sin is not always the main issue (see John 9:1-3 – the man born blind). There are a number of different types of healing that may be needed (see Appendix C).

- His friends lowered him through the roof and committed him into the hands of Jesus. When we seek healing, we need to commit ourselves to God and trust that he will give us the healing that we need, accepting that this is not always the healing that we want. Sometimes we may get both (as this man did). He may see our need for other sorts of healing as being of more importance than the sort of healing we want. We need to fundamentally put ourselves in his hands and commit ourselves to him.

- You may wish to include the issue of faith. Jesus saw the faith of the friends. Faith is often important in healing and is complete faith in Jesus and his power and love. The friends literally brought the man to Jesus' feet.

- Jesus proves his ability to forgive sin through his ability to physically heal. We have the same access to forgiveness through his death and resurrection. We can be made whole through his death on the cross where we can receive whatever healing we require. One way of seeking healing is to imagine ourselves going to the foot of the cross of Jesus and committing ourselves to his power and care there.

- You may also wish to point out that most illness is not due to sin, e.g. John 9:1-3.

Prayer:

Lord Jesus, thank you that you died and rose from the dead for every person present today. Thank you that through your death and resurrection, we can be made whole in you. We come together to the foot of your cross, committing ourselves to you, and asking that you heal us and make us whole. Amen.

Sermon 2: Healing from the past

Suggested passage: John 4:4-42 – Jesus and the Samaritan woman at the well.

- The woman had a difficult past which appeared to be causing social stigma and shame.
  - She was a Samaritan (disliked by the Jews), she was a woman, it was noon (people usually got water in the early mornings/late evenings – she was avoiding society), she was on her own, and Jesus breaks the social rules and asks her for a drink.
  - She had five husbands but the man she lived with then was not her husband. Why? Was she married as a teenager, widowed and then passed from brother to brother? Was she infertile and therefore unwanted? Was she disabled? Had she been abused?
- Women at that time did not have the right to divorce a man – the legal authority rested with the man alone. So it is unlikely that she chose the situation she was in. Worth noting that the passage does not say she was a prostitute.
- Her interaction with Jesus is transformative. He confronts her past, offers her living water, tells her who he is. As a result, she runs into the town and brings people out to Jesus. She effectively becomes an evangelist and brings many to Jesus.

- Jesus can transform us too but sometimes he needs to heal us of our past before we can go forward. We too may have a difficult past, which may include:
    - Sin, sinful habits and addictions
    - Painful memories
    - Difficult or abusive relationships
    - Unforgiveness towards others
    - Shame and anger. Perhaps anger with God.
- We may need to bring to him those things that we don't like to remember or think about so that he can bring us healing and wholeness and equip us for his service and the future.

Prayer:

Lord Jesus, we bring before you now all those present today. We bring to you the difficult, painful things and the struggles we have had. Shine your light on the hidden things of the past and bring us healing and wholeness from them through your death and resurrection. Amen.

Appendix B: Sermon suggestions

Sermon 3: The weapon of prayer

Suggested passage: Daniel 10:1-14 – Daniel's vision of a man.

- Daniel prayed. He prayed and mourned for three weeks. He went without choice food and wine and didn't use lotions. It appears that he prayed earnestly and fervently. How often do we pray persistently rather than a simple one-off prayer?

- Daniel's prayers produced a response – the angel came in response to them (v.12). Our prayers too may produce a response that we cannot see and do not know.

- The angel was detained for three weeks by the prince of Persia, generally thought to be an archdemon. After three weeks, Michael came to help. Daniel had prayed for three weeks until the angel was released, although he didn't know this. We do not know the power that our prayers have. Do we give up too easily? 2 Corinthians 10:4 says, "The weapons we fight with are not the weapons of the world. On the contrary, they have divine power to demolish strongholds."

- Sometimes, when we pray for healing and wholeness we may be unknowingly engaging in spiritual battles. Like Daniel, we need to be persistent and faithful in our prayers. Remember that Jesus has already secured victory through his death and resurrection.

Prayer:

Lord Jesus, thank you that you have already secured the ultimate victory over sin, sickness and death. Help us to take the power of prayer seriously and not to get discouraged if we don't see the immediate results we are hoping for. Amen.

Appendix C: Types of healing

There are several different types of healing that Jesus did and may occur when we pray for healing and wholeness. If the Holy Spirit shows us which type of healing is required, we can pray for it specifically. The "treatment" is different depending on the "diagnosis" – the underlying problem. Details about how to manage each is beyond the remit of this book, but it is helpful to understand some of the facets and problems that can impact on our wholeness. I have named seven types below:

1. Healing from sin – including sinful habits and addictions
2. Inner healing – healing from past hurts, emotional trauma, painful memories, the need to forgive others
3. Physical healing – healing of the body
4. Healing from demons – healing for those affected by demons
5. Healing from mental illness
6. Healing for relationships – healing our broken relationships with each other
7. Healing of our relationship with God

Just a footnote – the number and types of healing differ depending on who you listen to or read. Francis MacNutt named four in his original book on healing: sickness of the spirit due to sin, sickness of the emotions, sickness of the body, sickness due to demons. John Wimber, in his book *Power Healing*, names five. He has the same first three as Francis MacNutt but then adds mental illness to healing of the demonised and has an additional one of healing of the dead and dying – largely praying for comfort and strength for those dying but also, infrequently, raising from the dead. Certainly, there is overlap – for example, an addiction may be a symptom of difficult life experiences requiring inner healing.

I have separated mental illness from demonisation and added in healing for relationships, although accept the significant overlap between some of the categories. I've also added in a category of healing our relationship with God, as I think sometimes our relationship with him can suffer because of our anger and hurt at things he hasn't prevented, or times where we have felt he was silent or absent.

Appendix D: Glossary of spiritual gifts

I have adapted this list from Tyndale House Publishers:[12]

1. Administration – ability to help steer the church or ministry to a God-given goal
2. Apostle – sent to new places with the gospel. Also covers ability in leadership and spiritual advice
3. Discernment – ability to see the truth
4. Evangelism – ability to communicate the gospel
5. Exhortation – ability to support others in their Christian development
6. Faith – confidence in God
7. Giving – ability to give and share resources
8. Healing – ability to help make others whole
9. Helper – ability to support others to develop their gifting

---

12. https://www.tyndale.com/sites/unfoldingfaithblog/2019/10/01/a-quick-list-of-biblical-spiritual-gifts-which-gifts-exist-and-what-they-mean/ (accessed October 2024).

10. Hospitality – ability to make others feel welcome
11. Knowledge – ability to understand the Bible
12. Leadership – ability to lead a church or project to a God-given goal
13. Mercy – sensitivity and empathy for those suffering leading to compassion
14. Prophecy – ability to speak God's message to others. (I've used the word "pictures" in this book for my own experience of this)
15. Serving – ability to identify tasks and get them done
16. Speaking in tongues – supernatural ability to speak a God-given language
17. Teaching – skills to communicate the Bible effectively
18. Wisdom – ability to work out what needs to be done

Further reading

Books on healing and wholeness:

Edgar Bell, *Redemptive Healing* (UK: Gill Kimber, 2020)

An updated version of that which I have quoted in this book. As a parish priest in the Anglican church, Edgar had a powerful and miraculous gift for healing. This is a short book but full of gold.

Francis MacNutt, *The Practice of Healing Prayer: A How-To Guide for Catholics* (Maryland: The Word Among Us Press, 2010)

This is one of Francis MacNutt's excellent books on prayer for healing. Francis had a powerful and miraculous gift for healing. This book is a simple, straightforward and practical approach based both on years of experience as well as biblical understanding.

Francis MacNutt, *Healing* (Notre Dame, Indiana: Ave Maria Press, originally published 1974, revised edition 1999)

This is Francis MacNutt's original book on healing. Many other books on Christian healing and wholeness have used this book as a basis and is probably the one to read if you want a longer read.

John Wimber, *Power Healing* (New York: HarperCollins, 1987)

John Wimber's book on his discovery of his miraculous gift of healing and his journey to using it. He describes different types of healing and different approaches that are required. Also describes his journey to the UK in 1983 to pray for his close friend David Watson.

David Watson, *Fear No Evil* (London: Hodder & Stoughton, 1984)

A well-known preacher and writer, David tells his own story of metastatic bowel cancer and the treatment he had. This book describes his personal journey as it unfolds, the thousands of people in churches across the globe who prayed for him, his experience of prayer and laying on of hands by John Wimber, and his interrogation and understanding of the theology of illness. David died soon after completing the book.

Christy Wimber, *Wholeness* (Oxford: Lion Hudson, 2019)

This book draws on Christy's own experience of mental health issues and addiction and how the church supports (or doesn't support) those who struggle with these. It includes a chapter by Katharine Welby-Roberts on her experience of mental health issues with a church/Christian context. Christy also talks about seeing others healed but having to watch her own son struggle with non-healing.

Books on pain and suffering:

C.S. Lewis, *The Problem of Pain* (Dublin: HarperCollins, 1940)

A classic. C.S. Lewis starts with the premise that if God were both good and almighty, his creatures would be happy. However, we are not happy, and therefore God is either not good or not almighty or both. He then takes this apart, looking at divine omnipotence and goodness, human wickedness, the fall of man, hell, animal pain and heaven. Not a light read but a classic nonetheless.

Timothy Keller, *Walking With God Through Pain and Suffering* (London: Hodder & Stoughton, 2013)

A long read but thorough. Looks at the theology around pain and suffering and then strategies for people who are walking through times of difficulty.

Books on forgiveness:

R.T. Kendall, *Total Forgiveness* (London: Hodder & Stoughton, 2001)

Essential to much of wholeness is the need to be forgiven and to forgive others. This is a short book by R.T. and well worth a read.

Acknowledgements

I am absolutely indebted to many people for helping to bring this book to fruition. I particularly wish to thank:

My husband, Ian, for his patience and support throughout the whole process. As a priest in the Church of England, he tells me that Appendix B probably contains at least twelve sermons, not three.

My parents, Gill and Geoff Kimber, for checking through the theology, challenging my thinking in some areas and helping me out with the original Greek meanings of some words and verses.

My children, for their support ("Oh no – Mum's writing another book!").

Charlotte Nobbs, fabulous trainer and significant mentor to me in praying for others, for her challenge to make the book more useful for the whole church, rather than just a personal devotional.

Vanessa Norman and my aunty Lizzie for their thoughtful encouragement, support and help.

Sharon Simpson, for bringing some order to the chaos, including the suggestion to split the book into three parts.

All those at the Church of the Good Shepherd, Carshalton Beeches, UK, for test driving various versions as the book developed. Particularly to the Willmoor homegroup – Cheryl, Anthony, Mark, Margaret, Christine, Keith, Ben, Mandy, Eve, Martin and Lesley – for test driving the group discussions in our homegroup meetings.

Bibliography

Baptist Union of Great Britain (2021), "Introduction to Safeguarding Support for Baptist Churches", https://www.baptist.org.uk/Publisher/File.aspx?ID=279610 (accessed July 2024).

Catholic Safeguarding Standards Agency (2020), "The Eight National Safeguarding Standards", https://catholicsafeguarding.org.uk/resources/the-eight-national-safeguarding-standards/ (accessed July 2024).

Church of England (2017), "Promoting a Safer Church", https://www.churchofengland.org/sites/default/files/2017-11/promoting-a-safer-church-policy-notes.pdf (accessed July 2024).

Davison, Andrew, *Why Sacraments?* (London: SPCK, 2013).

MacNutt, Francis, *Healing* (Notre Dame, Indiana: Ave Maria Press, 1999).

MacNutt, Francis, *The Practice of Healing Prayer: A How-To Guide for Catholics* (Frederick, Maryland: The Word Among Us Press, 2010).

Tyndale House Publishers, "Your Spiritual Gifts – How to Identify and Effectively Use Them", https://www.tyndale.com/sites/unfoldingfaithblog/2018/11/13/your-spiritual-gifts-how-to-identify-and-effectively-use-them/ (accessed October 2024).

Wimber, John, and Springer, Kevin, *Power Healing* (New York: HarperCollins, 1987).

Printed in Dunstable, United Kingdom

64401519R00131